STUDENT BODY
OF LAW FOR TEXAS

Everything College Students Need to Know About the Law

STUDENT BODY OF LAW FOR TEXAS

SCOT COURTNEY

www.palaribooks.com

Student Body of Law for Texas© 2007, By Scot Courtney

Published by Palari Publishing
www.palaribooks.com

All rights reserved. No part of this book may be reproduced or utilized in any form or by any means, electronic or mechanical, including photocopying, recording or by any information storage and retrieval system, without permission in writing from the Publisher.

Inquiries should be addressed to: Permissions Department
Palari Publishing LLP, PO Box 9288, Richmond, VA 23227-0288

Library of Congress Cataloging-in-Publication Data

Courtney, Scot, 1965-
 Student body of law for Texas : everything college students need to know about the law / by Scot Courtney.
       p. cm.
 Includes index.
 ISBN-13: 978-1-928662-09-9 (pbk.)
 ISBN-10: 1-928662-09-9 (pbk.)
 1. Law--Texas--Popular works. 2. College students--Texas--Handbooks, manuals, etc. 3. Money management (budget) I. Title.
 KFT1282.C6C68 2007
 349.764--dc22

                                                                              2007008460

Printed in the United States of America
10 9 8 7 6 5 4 3 2 1

Cover design: Ted Randler
Interior: Zachary Abbott, Brian Bear
Editing: Catherine B. Saydlowski

This book is designed for general information only. The information presented at this site should not be construed to be formal legal advice or the formation of a lawyer/client relationship. Persons using this book are encouraged to seek independent counsel for advice regarding their individual legal issues.

This book is dedicated to:

My Wife, G,

for her love, support and her belief in me;

My Mother,

for my upbringing, love and instilling confidence in myself;

My Mentor, Robert Scardino,

for teaching me how to be an ethical & aggressive trial attorney.

TABLE OF CONTENTS

Chapter 1 - Introduction 1

Chapter 2 - Some Good Advice 4

Chapter 3 - Your Legal Rights 10

Chapter 4 - Crime & Punishment .25

Chapter 5 - Adult vs 21 47

Chapter 6 - "Let's Party!" 60

Chapter 7 - Self-Defense, Guns, & Weapons 108

Chapter 8 - Apartments, Leases, Housing 118

Chapter 9 - Transportation 130

Chapter 10 - Credit Cards, Banks & "Hot" Checks 154

Chapter 11 - Traveling Abroad .162

Chapter 12 - Guilt by Association 168

Chapter 13 - Just for the Women 179

        Conclusion 193

        Index 194

CHAPTER ONE
INTRODUCTION

If you are reading this, you are most likely in college, probably somewhere in Texas, therefore the book is written with certain assumptions. Unfortunately, our secondary educational system, fails to educate students in some very basic areas that may impact you now and for the rest of your life. Really basic concerns are covered in this book to give you a rudimentary understanding of the law, how it works or doesn't work, and how it can and will impact your life. As you can see, the table of contents tries to give you the framework of areas I will discuss and gives quick reference for those of you that have fallen into the time-honored, but deplorable habit of failing to read the entire book. That's OK. I've been there and that's exactly why I have written this book the way I have. Many of the areas covered, I learned in college the hard way. Some I learned afterwards in law school or during my years of criminal law practice. Others I only recently discovered when researching and writing this book. Almost every time, whether long ago or just yesterday, my usual reaction was "Really? I didn't realize that." or "Oh, crap!" whichever the case may be.

Knowledge is power: the more you know, the better prepared you are to deal with whatever situation in which you may find yourself.

Knowledge is power, the more you know, the better prepared you are to deal with whatever situation in which you may find yourself. I hope that this book answers those questions before you are presented with a problem and can help you get through your college years without those "life experiences" so many of us had to endure. While college involves more than just scholarly pursuits, and many of the things that will happen during those years will distract you from your studies, if you are armed with a little bit of knowledge, you may very well steer clear of the "life experiences" that can be rather unpleasant. Even if you cannot

The Student Body of Law

avoid them, you will be better equipped to deal with those situations to minimize any adverse affects. In any event, this book is meant to help you get through it all.

Another concern while in college is money. I, myself, did not have much and was always looking for ways to get by on a budget, if you could call it that. So I have written this book with this in mind with the hope that the information may ultimately save you some bucks along the way. If money is not a problem, please excuse those passages; some of us need the help.

Likewise, this book deals with some areas that don't seem fair or right. I'm not telling you what is right or wrong, just what the law says. If you don't like it, please take the opportunity to write your representatives in both Washington D.C. and in Austin or the legislature in your state. Moral judgments, religious concerns, or feelings of guilt and self-doubt will not enter into the posture of this book. I am an attorney and leave such areas to those who have an expertise in their areas, such as priests, psychiatrists, rabbis, psychologists, pastors, ministers, or whomever you personally rely on for such areas of concern.

This book is not intended to be legal advice, but merely an overview of certain laws, legal terms, and areas that may, or may not address your exact and particular question(s). The real intent is to arm you with information that will keep you out of trouble, before you find yourself in it.

There are many variations and exceptions to all of these areas and it is strongly suggested that if you are unsure about what you should do in a particular situation, contact an attorney for legal advice or contact the legal services office at your local university. Most universities have legal counsel on staff or can refer you to a lawyer that will not charge you for simple advice or counsel. Most local lawyers will welcome the opportunity to at least discuss your problem or make suggestions without charging you one penny.

MEET JOE BUTTHEAD

Generally speaking, *don't* be like Joe.

If Joe were a real person, he'd definitely be a permanent resident of the Texas prison system by now.

Throughout this book, I'll refer to a fellow by the name of "Joe Butthead." Joe for short. You'll get to know our pal Joe real well over the coming pages, if you don't know him by some other name already. In this book, he's not based on one actual person, but rather is an amalgam of many guys I knew in college, good and bad. I use him instead of the names of those that actually committed the alleged crimes, behavior and activities detailed or referenced throughout this book. He is used to illustrate and better demonstrate how the facts of a situation may be applied to the law and the various possible interpretations of the law. If Joe were a real person, he'd definitely be a permanent resident of the Texas prison system by now. Generally speaking, don't be like Joe. Use his bad manners and decision-making abilities to avoid the mistakes he makes throughout this book.

He's not based on one actual person, but rather is an amalgam of many guys I knew in college, good...

...and **bad**.

CHAPTER TWO
SOME GOOD ADVICE
A PRIMER ON MANNERS, CUSTOM AND DECORUM WHEN "DEALING WITH THE COPS."

I think everyone can agree that one of the hardest, most stressful, and dangerous jobs in the world is being a police officer. They have to deal with people that most of us would never want to meet in any situation, much less at times and in places that are just plain scary. The vast majority of these officers are ethical and mindful of both the U.S Constitution and the basic concept of fairness. They serve their communities and are an essential cog in our society's peaceful and safe operation.

That being said, the problem, as it is with any profession, is that a few bad cops can make it bad for the whole bunch, at least as it appears generally. There are officers out there that may bring with them to their jobs insecurities, control issues, anger management problems, or are just in it for the pure power surge the job gives them. These are some practical tips to employ, not only to reduce your chances for arrest, but also to ensure that all those other officers performing their duty properly are afforded the respect and dignity they deserve from you. These tips are offered keeping in mind your rights afforded you under both the U.S. and Texas Constitutions, which are discussed later. You must decide how to handle yourself and how far you are willing to go to cooperate with police officers, keeping in mind what consequences your cooperation or lack of thereof may result.

Always be respectful of officers you come into contact with, either on

The vast majority of these officers are ethical and mindful of both the U.S Constitution and the basic concept of fairness.

the street or otherwise. A good policy of "Yes Sir/No Sir" without the "Eddie Haskell" attitude will serve you well. Don't offer small talk or excuses, just answer the officer's questions and peacefully comply with his/her requests. Don't cop an attitude that you are being inconvenienced or argue the law with the officer; he or she will not appreciate it and may decide that you need to be taught a lesson — a lesson that requires a night in jail to teach you some manners.

Don't cop an attitude that you are being inconvenienced or argue the law with the officer; he or she will not appreciate it and may decide that you need to be taught a lesson — a lesson that requires a night in jail to teach you some manners.

You have a much better chance of being sent on your way if you exhibit through your actions and responses to the officer that you are a law-abiding, polite, reasonable, and safe individual. This minimizes your chances of going to jail and/or being accused of a crime.

According to the Texas Department of Public Safety, when stopped by a law enforcement officer, DPS recommends that you:

1) Keep your hands in plain sight;
2) Cooperate fully with the police officer;
3) If you have a gun with you, tell the officer as soon as possible;
4) Don't make any quick movements, especially toward the weapon; and,
5) At night, turn on your vehicle's dome light.

I tend to agree with most of this advice, but I will leave it to you to decide what is and is not good advice based upon your reading of the upcoming portions of this book.

Never physically resist or avoid an officer's grasp or interfere with an officer's actions, much less strike an officer. These actions will most likely result in additional charges of either Resisting Arrest (See Tex. Penal Code Sec. 38.03), which is a Class A Misdemeanor; or Third Degree Felony if a "weapon" is used, and could result in your suffering physical harm yourself. If force is used against the officer, you could be charged with Assault of a Peace Officer, a Third Degree Felony (See Tex. Penal Code Sec. 22.01); or

The Student Body of Law

Aggravated Assault of a Peace Officer, a First Degree Felony (See Tex. Penal Code Sec. 22.02) if a weapon is used. Historically speaking, such situations can be extremely volatile and have even resulted in someone's death at the hands of the arresting officers.

Obviously avoiding an officer or erratic driving will result in your being stopped and questioned for something, if for nothing else than your "suspicious" behavior. Immediately walking away or running when a cop pulls up is a sure-fire way to get run down and "detained" for questioning.

Never run away. You definitely run the risk of being charged with Evading Detention or Arrest, a Class B Misdemeanor. If it involves a vehicle, it's a Felony with escalating degrees of punishment ranges for various "police chase" situations, including a Second Degree Felony if someone is killed as a result of your flight or escape, depending on the offense for which the person has been arrested. There is also the possibility that the officers giving chase may decide to and be authorized to use deadly force to apprehend you. This means they might be justified in shooting you.

Don't step in to help out your buddy who has just been arrested, much less help him break the chains of bondage and run away. You expose yourself to the possibility of joining your friend in the back seat of the cop car. You will not be seen as a help to the officers, but rather as an obstruction. You could be arrested for several offenses, including Permitting or Facilitating Escape, a Second Degree Felony (See Tex. Penal Code Sec. 38.07) or Hindering Apprehension or Prosecution, Class A Misdemeanor (See Tex. Penal Code Sec. 38.05). The best thing you can do for your friend is contact the jail and try to bail him out first thing in the morning.

Don't be like Joe: "You can beat the rap, but you can't beat the ride."

Don't make a bad situation worse. It is not a defense to any of the above-detailed offenses that the arrest itself was a false arrest. Try to minimize your potential criminal exposure. Remember, the old saying, "You can beat the rap, but you won't beat the ride." You may ask, "What the hell does that mean?" It means that whether or not you may ultimately be convicted of whatever crime you have been arrested, you will nonetheless suffer the experiences of humiliation, degradation, and inconvenience that comes with spending a night in jail.

COPS & THEIR AUTHORITY

All peace officers are held to the same requirements, generally, the U.S. Constitution as to how they can intrude upon and pry into a citizen's life. Law enforcement officers include any and all peace officers, game wardens, constables, sheriffs, deputies, TABC officers, as well as Federal Agents, such as FBI, DEA, Customs, Immigration and Homeland Security, although that last one seems to be debatable if there are any constitutional restrictions. State police officers may be further restricted by state constitutions, but generally the U.S. Constitution gives us the best and most reliable guidepost.

A popular misconception is that officers outside their geographic jurisdiction lose their authority as peace officers. In Texas, any certified peace officer has authority to act in the capacity of a peace officer anywhere in the state and is considered under the law to always be "on duty", whether actually "on duty" or not. It does not extend beyond the state line, however a federal agent's jurisdiction extends throughout the U.S.

WHERE DOES THE LAW COME FROM?

Austin!! The weirdest town in Texas, Home of the Longhorns, 6th Street, Live Music, Bats, and our beautiful State Capital. By the way, our capitol building has the largest and tallest dome of any state capitol, even bigger than the U.S. Capitol building in D.C. Every two years, our elected representatives in the Texas Senate and Texas House of Representatives meet in Austin to amend the law we have and create new law they think we need. Every now and then they repeal one or two. Our federal government in Washington, D.C. does this same thing, but our state laws affect us more directly. Since this book deals mainly with Texas law, we'll stick to that. If you want a good explanation of how a law becomes a law, I refer you to the short Saturday morning cartoon from the '70's *Schoolhouse Rock* series. That's how I learned how a bill becomes a law.

The Student Body of Law

We have a vast body of laws, probably too many, codified in the different sections of the Texas Code and other administrative regulations, all of which generally come from the politicians in Austin. The laws that are actually written down are considered "black letter" or "statutory" law; how the laws have been applied, reviewed and interpreted by the courts is considered "common law".

If you get wind of a proposed law going into affect or have a problem with one already enacted, send a letter or e-mail to your representative and senator and let them know, respectfully, how you feel and why. Don't be shy, it's your right and just one way that your voice can be heard in the system.

LAWYERS
"I NEED A LAWYER, BUT I DON'T KNOW ANY"

The best way to find a good and reputable attorney is by referral. Hopefully you know an attorney that can refer you to a good lawyer that practices in the area of need. If you don't know an attorney, maybe you know someone who does and that is a good way to start. You may have to talk to a few people and be referred several times, but keep at it until you find someone that can and, most importantly, wants to help you. Surf the net. If no other option is available and you're desperate, the yellow pages will do, but let's think about some other options before you start your fingers walking. Ask around. Your friends, professors you can talk to, co-workers, and family should at least give you a start.

Most universities have legal counsel available on-campus that can answer many questions you may have and in some instances, even represent you. This is another good source of information and they can also refer you to a good local attorney you can talk with.

"HOW DO I FIND A GOOD ONE?"

A good rule of thumb is to get a few names, make appointments, and go talk to several different attorneys before writing a check. Don't just talk to one — there are plenty of attorneys out there — so find one you are comfortable with. If you get a letter from an attorney in the mail after an arrest, I suggest you throw it away; I have never heard a positive story from someone that hired one of these "cut rate" lawyers. Any reputable attorney should at least be willing to give you a few minutes of their time for free. If not, they are probably too busy to devote their time to your case, to your satisfaction, so move on.

Ask plenty of questions. If the lawyer can't answer your questions, or at least give you a good reason why they can't, move on. Remember, if it sounds too good to be true, it probably is. Any lawyer that guarantees you the outcome of any case cannot be trusted. They are either lying to you or involved in something you don't want to be involved in. That goes for price also. You get what you pay for. Be very circumspect of an attorney that charges a fee substantially lower than those you have talked with. Sometimes, your pocketbook makes these decisions, but always consider all aspects of the case — your budget, your priorities and expectations — not only in the immediate future, but long-term. This is another good reason to talk with several different attorneys so you can get an idea of what the market pricing is and make your choices accordingly.

CRIMINAL ALLEGATIONS & THE UNIVERSITY

Many Texas universities have stringent rules and policies regarding how a criminal allegation may affect the student's education. Problems with the university administration are usually exacerbated if the offense alleged occurred "on campus". Some universities have extremely harsh consequences, especially if there is a strict student code. If you are charged or arrested for a crime, you may also be charged with a complaint for violating a student conduct code, if your school complies with such. These types of complaints are generally submitted in writing to student government or a university disciplinary committee for resolution. Disciplinary actions may include suspension, dismissal, expulsion, or letters of reprimand. Defending your criminal charges may, therefore, be only half the battle. You should become quite familiar with your school's policies and get a copy of the student handbook or code of conduct to understand your rights "on campus" and the procedures for fighting any harmful actions taken against you. They can usually be found on-line.

CHAPTER THREE
Your Legal Rights
"AS SEEN ON TV"

So you have been stopped, arrested, charged or otherwise investigated for the commission of a crime. What are your rights and what can you do. First off, we will go through the typical "Miranda Warning" that everyone has heard a hundred times in the movies and on TV.

"You are under arrest for (insert charge); you have the right to remain silent; anything you say or do may be and most likely will be used against you at a trial for this or any other offense; you have the right to an attorney, if you cannot afford an attorney, one will be provided for you; you may give up these rights and speak to an officer."

There are hundreds of variations of this warning, but the gist of it is to let you know that you are under arrest and you do not have to say or do anything. You can refuse to answer questions at any time, even if you are stopped in your car or walking down the street.

A popular misconception is that if the police have not "read you your rights," their failure to do so will somehow negatively impact the arrest. It may affect what evidence may be admissible in court, namely statements made by you in response to questioning, but, all in all, that is the only significant effect this failure may have. That's not to say that a good trial attorney won't use such a breach in policy and protocol to your advantage at trial, but it probably won't get your case thrown out of court.

IN THE REAL WORLD
IS IDENTIFICATION REQUIRED?

State statutes that require a citizen to disclose their name when requested by a law enforcement officer, known as "stop and identify" statutes have been held constitutional by the U.S. Supreme Court. Basically, the Court determined that such a law or an officer's request for identity was constitutionally valid, so long as it was in relation to the purpose, rationale, and practical demands of the initial stop. Also important is that the request for identification was reasonably related in scope to the circumstances that justified the stop, and that the citizen's statement in response, is not incriminating.

Texas has no such statute, BUT, if you have been detained, but not arrested by a police officer, you don't have to give them squat. However, refusing to identify yourself might cause them to arrest you anyway and take you downtown so they can determine who you really are. You are not legally required to carry a driver's license or other ID if you're not driving, but it is a crime to give false information about your identity, whether you've been arrested or just detained. If you've been arrested, you do have to give your name, address, and date of birth to a police officer who requests it. They'll probably ask you for lots more than this, but these three items are all you're legally required to give. You are merely required to identify yourself, usually by producing a driver's license or ID card, if an officer requests, but that is about it. If you do answer questions, remember, whatever you say may very well, and probably will be, used as evidence later.

Basically, the best policy is once you are under arrest, which means, that you are not free to leave or are actually restrained, you probably should not say anything other than to identify yourself and request to speak with an attorney.

YOUR RIGHT TO REMAIN SILENT

The 5th Amendment to the U.S. Constitution guarantees that a no person "shall be compelled in any criminal case to be a witness against himself." This area of law has evolved into an area with many exceptions and nuances, as have all others, but generally speaking, any statement made by a person who is in custody and in response to custodial interrogation (questions by the police while under arrest) cannot be used against a person, unless they have been informed of their rights and they waive those rights. Any statement made, with or without the warning, that is not in response to a question is not protected. Basically, the best policy is once you are under arrest, which means, that you are not free to leave or are actually restrained, you probably should not say anything other than to identify yourself and request to speak with an attorney. This also applies to other people, such as others who are under arrest, whom you may feel compelled to "tell your story" to while in

The Student Body of Law

jail or the back seat of the patrol car.

If the police officers or investigators become aggressive or threaten you, remain resolute in your determination not to answer their questions. They're not there "to help you," nor do they have any authority to "make you a deal" or "go easy on you." Only the prosecutor has the authority to do so, so don't fall for their trap. The U.S. Supreme Court has held that it is okay for the police to lie to you and trick you into talking, making statements or "confessing." They still can't beat you, at least for now, nor can they subject you to coercion such as withholding food, water, or other essentials for life, but they can make it extremely uncomfortable and unpleasant, so your best bet and quickest way out of the interrogation situation is to continue to refuse to answer any questions and ask for an attorney in a polite and respectful manner, repeatedly if necessary. (See the **I WANNA TALK TO MY ATTORNEY** section on the page 14.)

This affects most people in the early stages of DWI at the initial stop and detention, which is discussed later, as well as during the investigatory stages of any criminal allegations.

The 5th Amendment also applies to trials. The choice of whether to testify or not is up to the person accused and they cannot be called by the state to testify against themselves. A person who has been subpoenaed to testify as a witness does not have the right not to testify, unless they have a privilege not to. There are certain privileges for spouses, doctors, reporters, and attorney/client communications. All of these privileges have exceptions, and if you find yourself in such a position, you should seek the advice of a reputable attorney in the field. Typically, a person who is asked questions that may incriminate themselves may assert their "5th Amendment Right" not to answer.

WHY NOT JUST EXPLAIN & THEY'LL LET ME GO?

They might, but don't bank on it. For those of you that have asked this question, God love you for your trusting soul, but I am here to tell you, statements made just after arrest, during police questioning and sometimes at trial from the witness chair, can be some of the most damning evidence, and when the person said it, they thought nothing of how it may be taken or how it sounded at the time.

There are some things that you need to understand:

1) The people that have stopped you are questioning you and/or have arrested you (the cops) are already convinced that you have done something illegal;
2) Because of this belief, they will probably not believe what you have to say, unless, of course, it helps to confirm their belief;
3) They are there to gather evidence against you;
4) You will probably see them at your trial later and they will not be there to testify for you;
5) At trial, even a marginal prosecutor can make a defendant look bad through good cross-examination;
6) The courtroom is like a big auditorium or public speech in front of a big audience; a witness can make a bad impression on the jury for any number of reasons, such as: nervousness, anxiety, shyness, a speech disorder, lack of education, cockiness, attitude, or any number of factors that may justify a defendant's reason not to testify other than his/her guilt.

I GOT A SUBPOENA

A right afforded to the prosecution, parties to civil lawsuits and the accused citizen is the right to compulsory process, which means the right and power to call and make witnesses appear and testify. A subpoena is the legal instrument that makes this happen. It is a common misconception that a subpoena has no "legal" affect unless it is actually placed in one's hands. This is not the case. There are various ways that a person can be forced to appear and testify pursuant to a subpoena, especially criminal and/or Grand Jury subpoenas. Certified mail, faxes, informing the person via telephone, and other methods have been ruled adequate, so if you have received or been informed of a subpoena requiring your attendance against your wishes, consult an attorney to discuss your options, as well as the testimony that is being sought.

Ignoring a subpoena is not the smart thing to do. If a witness does not appear as ordered by the subpoena, the issuing party may ask the Court or Grand Jury to attach the witness, which means, they issue a warrant for arrest to hold the person in custody until their testimony is needed.

The Student Body of Law

"I WANNA TALK TO MY LAWYER"
RIGHT TO A LAWYER

You certainly have the right to legal counsel at any time that you choose. This does not mean that after the police officer has arrested you that they will immediately take you by your Dad's attorney's office or hand you their cell phone to give him a call. Even if you continue to ask for an attorney, you may not actually get to talk with one for several hours, if not longer.

THE BAD NEWS

The practical problem most often times is that you are not free to just pick up the phone, because you are being arrested AND it's 2am in the morning AND you know your Dad's golfing buddy, Mr. Cheatham, the lawyer, is fast asleep AND the cops know this AND they don't really care AND they would rather have you on videotape extremely pissed off and irrational, rather than poised and courteous. It's a bit of a "Catch 22" in that you may request an attorney, but they don't have to let you have one or talk to one for quite some time.

THE GOOD NEWS

The good news is that your request to speak with an attorney may affect what they do or don't do with you and may affect the admissibility of any statements you make after that point. Very similar to the Right to Remain Silent section discussed above, the basic rule is that once you inform the arresting police officer or an investigating agent knocking on your door or other similar state official, that you either wish to speak with an attorney before going further or advise them to direct all communications to your attorney, they should not continue with any form of questioning that may illicit any responses that may incriminate you. Remember to be courteous and respectful, but resolute in your decision not to answer their questions. Request to speak with an attorney, repeatedly if necessary, if you decide to exercise these rights.

The real issue is: when is it legally required that you be afforded an attorney. If you have been arrested, have not been released on bail, and can't afford an attorney, you have the right to an attorney provided to you to represent you, including at trial. Some courts have begun to take the position that if a person has made bail they can afford to hire an attorney. This is not the law and any person has the right to have an attorney provided, if they are indigent and cannot afford one.

FREE SPEECH

You wander into your local coffee house one morning and it is there you first see her. Long dark hair, unmade, Elvis Costello glasses, sipping coffee, while she apathetically reads the local campus rag. Disgusted with the world, she tosses her paper on the table and trudges out. Over the next few weeks you hang at the coffee house until you find an opportunity to talk to her and BANG, you're in love.

Lola is her name, this really cool, beautiful, dark, loud, in-your-face, pissed off at the world, political chick that likes you and she has convinced you that fur and leather wearers, as well as meat eaters, are all evil and must be stopped. Lola has convinced you through advanced brainwashing techniques such as prolonged periods of wild sex, that you should help her and her vegan friends when they decide to mount a protest in the Quad. You arrive at the appointed time and begin to voice your (her) opinions regarding the evils of fur, meat and even leather goods. Lola then hands you a bucket of red paint and instructs you to voice those same opinions while hurling red paint on each person that walks by wearing leather or fur. Just for good measure, someone whips out a US flag and begins to burn it. You've got quite a protest going on when the campus police arrive and the kiss of steel wraps around your wrists. BANG, you're under arrest. But why? Protest and free speech is the only way to bring about social change and raise the public consciousness. All true, but as you will see, absolute protection is not guaranteed. You may be facing charges ranging from Criminal Mischief, Assault, Inciting a Riot, as well as breaking other similar ordinances and campus rules and regulations.

FIRST AMENDMENT

I'm not telling you that public protest and speech are not a good thing. As matter of fact, free speech, the expression of ideas, and civic protest are just a few of my favorite things and are valid and legal ways to make your opinions known. All I'm trying to get across to you is that there are some limitations on the way that you go about it, at least to avoid a trip to the local jail. If your message is that important, find a way to lawfully express it. If not, I admire

The Student Body of Law

your convictions, if not the message.

Congress shall make no law respecting an establishment of religion, or prohibiting the free exercise thereof; or abridging the freedom of speech, or of the press; or the right of the people peaceably to assemble, and to petition the Government for a redress of grievances. — The First Amendment to the U.S. Constitution

Without the First Amendment, religious minorities could be persecuted, protesters could be forcibly silenced, the press could not criticize the government, and the citizens could not demand or effect social change.

School-sponsored prayer, the Pledge of Allegiance, and the removal of religious figures or the Ten Commandments from public buildings are just a couple of issues we see in the media that impacts the rights of free speech and religion. Religious liberty and toleration are constantly pitted against conflicting religious beliefs, the law, or a citizen's right to be free from forced exposure to another citizen's religious practice or beliefs. Historically, other issues have come and gone, but the hallmark to resolving these issues, ironically, is the freedom itself: the right to freely express and debate one's views, contribute to the ultimate resolution, whatever the resolution may be. These sorts of difficulties are the price of freedom of speech and religion in a tolerant, open society. But, are we as a nation as tolerant as we like to think?

The Supreme Court has never said that all speech is protected, but political speech apparently enjoys the most protection, while commercial and obscene speech have a lesser degree of freedom. A citizen does not have a right to say anything at any time in any place. In some instances, what is or is not "speech" is an important element in determining the degree of freedom associated with the speech, but also it is the distinction between speech and conduct that may impact Supreme Court decisions interpreting these issues. Speech that is part of an otherwise illegal act enjoys no protection and "hate speech" continues to draw the eye of the Supreme Court each October.

A MODERN HISTORY OF FREE SPEECH

The first freedoms guaranteed in the Bill of Rights are the forty-five words of the First Amendment written by James Madison, signed and adopted in 1787, but not actually in effect until 1791. It was a relatively radical idea to allow citizens the freedom to question, ridicule, call for change, or otherwise openly debate the actions of those in power. This right would help protect the citizenry from governmental oppression by allowing the citizen to question its own government's action or inaction. The First Amendment was the response to the citizens' demand for a guarantee of their basic freedoms; you too should continually demand the same. A short modern history will help you understand the evolution of how this right has been exercised in the twentieth century.

In the early years of the twentieth century leading up to "The Great War," increasing internal opposition and debate about America's involvement in the First World War cropped-up, and as U.S. involvement increased, organizations formed to voice some relatively unpopular opinions against U.S. involvement. This type of "unpopular free speech" spawned debate regarding a citizen's right to speak out against the government at all. Other issues, such as: the draft, the use of the mail to distribute anti-war/anti-draft literature, and restricting speech encouraging men to resist the draft intensified the debate. The American Union Against Militarism (AUAM) was formed, among others that publicly questioned the policies of the U.S. government. During this period of national "insecurity," the government sought to suppress the voices that questioned the government's policies. More fundamentally alarming was the official government suppression of the protests and speech itself.

The First Amendment was the response to the citizens' demand for a guarantee of their basic freedoms; you too should continually demand the same.

The federal government's response to the gathering momentum opposing U.S. involvement was the passing of the Espionage Act in 1917, which made it a crime to "willfully obstruct the recruiting or enlistment service of the United States." The Sedition Act of 1918 were amendments to the earlier legislation adding "disloyal" or "abusive" criticism of the government as illegal activity. The Postal Service even got into the act by banning anti-war and anti-draft propaganda from the mail, even confiscating the mail of suspect organizations.

In order to focus on the protection of free speech during the war, the AUAM created the National Civil Liberties Bureau (NCLB) in 1917. The NCLB drew the most fire from the government in its attempts to silence the NCLB's voice. After the war, the NCLB became the American Civil Liberties

The Student Body of Law

Union (ACLU) in 1920. Although a misconception in this writer's view, the popular, contemporary view of the ACLU is that of the ultra-liberal rabid dog, poised to attack any and all restrictions on expression. No matter your personal view, the ACLU is a perfect example of the need for organizations and citizens to exercise the Constitution to challenge the majority or "popular" view and protect the rights of those that may hold an unpopular opinion, ultimately protecting the majority's right to profess its "popular" opinions. In order to achieve this, one must grit his teeth and bear the opposition in order to be able to voice his own.

Our government has committed vast and significant violations of citizens rights and civil liberties. The government's response to WWI opposition first illustrated in the early part of the century; the deportation of thousands for their political views during the "Red Scare" of the '20s; our government's internment of thousands of American Citizens of Japanese descent in remote camps during WWII; the McCarthyism "Red Scare" blacklist "witch hunts" of the '50s; and the killing of college student protesters at Kent State in the '60s, are all poignant examples that illustrate that in times of national stress, real or imagined, First Amendment rights come under enormous pressure, sometimes resulting in public paranoia, and result in our government trampling on citizens' rights in the name of security.

As the century progressed, "unpopular" speakers began to enjoy greater protection by the courts. State and local restrictions were struck down and the range of protected speech expanded. The end of the 20th Century witnessed a resurgence in calls for censorship to combat the "evils" associated with pop-culture, music, film, video games, and media content. Many believe that with the events of 9/11 and the passing of the Patriot Act and similar legislation, our country is entering into another era that threatens to further restrict citizens' rights.

The issue of restriction of speech on college campuses has been especially active in the past twenty years and many colleges have in place restrictions that have great limitations on public speech and expression. Check your school's rules and policies before taking to the streets. If you feel that those restrictions infringe on your rights, make your voice heard and try to change them. If not, go get your message out.

Back to the really cool, beautiful, dark, loud, in-your-face, political chick, known later in this book as Crazy Lola. Although her message may ring true to your ears, try to find ways to make your point without trampling on the rights of other citizens, especially on campus. Maybe read some of the writings and teachings of Mahatma Ghandi regarding passive resistance, or Dr. Martin Luther Kings' writings on civil disobedience and non-violent protest. They were quite effective in bringing about great social and political change in relatively short periods of time. Be committed to your beliefs, but remember to listen to others, and most importantly, respect their right to hold, debate, disagree, and express those opinions with which you disagree.

SEARCH AND SEIZURE

Any restriction in a citizen's freedom of movement or detention by the government is an arrest, or rather a seizure, of one's person. A search is any intrusion into a citizens "zone of privacy," that is, any area in which a reasonable citizen may expect privacy from the public. Any arrest or search of a citizen is considered unreasonable unless the officers conducting the arrest and/or search have Probable Cause to do so.

PROBABLE CAUSE AND REASONABLE SUSPICION

The reasonable suspicion requirement is just one of many 'checks' that help to ensure that citizens are not subjected to unreasonable searches and seizures as protected by the Fourth Amendment and the Texas Constitution. Before an officer can stop and detain a person, the officer must have Reasonable Suspicion (specific articulable facts to reasonably suspect that the person stopped is associated with criminal activity).

YOUR CAR

 In order to search someone's vehicle, an officer must have Probable Cause (PC), which is defined as facts and circumstances within the officer's knowledge reasonably trustworthy to lead a person of reasonable caution and prudence to believe that the officer will find the instrumentality of a crime, or that the person arrested is connected to criminal activity.

   We see Joe Butthead cruising down the road in his 1988 Dodge Diplomat, with the NORML sticker on the bumper, dark-tinted windows and red tape covering one of the cracked taillights. Joe is headed to pick up his date for dinner and a movie. Joe has his favorite Kid Rock CD blaring and the windows rolled down. As Joe rolls through the stop sign that no one ever stops at, a police cruiser's lights flash in Joe's rearview. He immediately pulls over to a safe place, signaling of course, and comes to a stop. The officer has

The Student Body of Law

Although Joe doesn't personally smoke the noxious weed himself, Joe's roommate regularly borrows the "sweet ride" for dates and has been know to "blow a bone" every now and then.

reasonable suspicion to stop Joe (the stop sign violation), but the reality is that the NORML sticker, the loud music, and the tinted windows probably didn't help Joe slide by without a second look either. Joe is smart and follows all the advice discussed in Chapter 2, but the officer still asks him to step out of the car. Joe complies and the officer now asks him a series of questions, like "You been drinkin'?", "What's your hurry?", "Where you going?" "You got anything in your car that I need to know about? Drugs, or guns?", and "You mind if I look in your car?". At this point, bells and whistles should be going off in Joe's head. Although Joe doesn't personally smoke the noxious weed himself, Joe's roommate regularly borrows the "sweet ride" for dates and has been know to "blow a bone" every now and then.

It is at this point Joe considers his options:
1) If Joe gives consent to search his car, whatever is found can be used against him;
2) If Joe refuses, the only way the officer can legally search is if he has probably cause and/or reasonable suspicion to do so; but
3) If the officer smells or claims later to have smelled "a distinct odor, that through his training and experience smells like burnt or burning marijuana" then he probably has PC or knows how to create PC to search Joe's car, otherwise he would have to get a warrant to search or have some justification to arrest Joe.

Lo and behold, he finds a "roach" or "extinguished marijuana cigarette" in the ashtray or under the seat where your moronic stoned roommate missed throwing it out the window the last time he borrowed your car. BANG, Joe is under arrest for Class B Misdemeanor Possession of Marijuana.

If you loan your car to your stoner friends, you better keep it clean, or you may pay for their fun with a night in the pokey. The real moral of the story is, if you choose to express yourself through the appearance of your car, expect to get pulled over more often than the mini-van your mom drives. Scrape the NORML sticker off, turn down the Kid Rock and make sure your inspection and registration stickers are valid, as well as all lights, license plate, and other reasons that may give an officer reason to stop you for anything. Maybe even make a donation to the local police officer association. They usually give you one of those "I support the Badge" type of window decals; stick it on, you need all the help you can get.

YOUR HOUSE AND HOME

Generally speaking, an officer cannot enter your home without your permission, without either a search or arrest warrant. If the officer sees something in plain view that constitutes a crime, the officer may enter. This situation usually comes up when an officer is dispatched to a loud music complaint. The officer knocks on the door. Joe Butthead opens the door and a cloud of smoke bellows out. The officer sees behind Joe his buddies sitting around the living room with a bong on the coffee table. In this situation, the officer may enter, seize the contraband (bong, marijuana, etc) and generally may arrest whomever he determines possessed the contraband — maybe everyone.

"I THINK I'LL JUST INVITE A FEW PEOPLE OVER"

Great idea. Lets say that Joe has a party, it is huge — people in and out spilling into the yard, cars parked up and down both sides of the street. The cops show up and barge into the house, whereupon they see alcohol being consumed and several under aged girls drinking, not to mention the half-smoked joint on the kitchen table. Issues may arise as to the officers' entry into the house, and generally it would be considered unreasonable. However, the presence of so many people freely entering and exiting the house and the underaged drinking will probably give rise to the prosecution's argument that Joe's house was open to the public and therefore the officers merely entered into a public space.

Now let's say that Joe's next party is not quite so big and is contained entirely inside the house. The cops show up and knock on the door. Joe answers the door and the cops tell him the music is too loud and asks if they can enter. Joe says "no, you can't enter, but I will turn down the music." The cops come inside anyway. The cops are not authorized in this situation and any evidence they seize or arrest may be subject to exclusion or legal attack and suppression.

Same situation as before, but when Joe tells the cops "no," they tell Joe, "You should let us in, otherwise we will get a warrant and come back in thirty minutes." That may or may not be true. In any event, the cops will probably not be able to get a warrant based upon the information they have. They must have Probable Cause to support the warrant, which in this situation does not appear to be present. Joe is certainly under no obligation to allow the officers in and if he does consent to let them in and they find something that exposes Joe to criminal prosecution, Joe cannot later complain that the officers didn't have a warrant because Joe consented to letting the cops inside with his permission.

Only a person who has a possessory interest in a house or car can give consent to enter to search. That means that a person who owns, rents, or is a guest actually staying in a house, apartment, or hotel room all have a possessory interest in the property and can consent to a search or entry.

CONSENT TO SEARCH? JUST SAY "NO"!

You have a constitutional right to say "no" to any officer who asks for your permission to search you, your car or your residence. Remember, once an officer has your permission to enter, whatever they see in plain view is fair game. Sometimes a refusal will bring threats to get a warrant or drug dog, but if the officer really had probable cause to search, he would search without even asking. Unless you are willing to waive any future complaint that the search resulted in finding illegal items, put the officer to the test and refuse them permission. If a search is reasonable under the law, an officer does not require your permission to search, but once your permission is given, the search is lawful, even without probable cause. All evidence obtained by a lawful search may be admissible against you. When in doubt as to whether you should consent to a search, just say "no."

Why should you say "no" to a request to search when you have nothing to hide? A reasonable search is based on an officer's knowledge that probable cause existed prior to the search and seizure. Your permission justifies the search, even an unreasonable search, but your refusal places the burden on the officer to demonstrate in court that the officer knew enough to justify a reasonable search before the search was conducted. Always remember that not all police officers are trustworthy and they have been known to stretch the truth on occasion to make arrests and convictions.

Reasonable searches and seizures are: 1) authorized by lawfully issued search warrants; 2) incidental to lawful arrests; and/or, 3) conducted with the voluntary express and specific consent.

Cops are not required to inform you that you have a constitutional right to refuse to allow a search and a refusal cannot be used to imply probable cause of criminal activity. Most times, officers are not really looking for anything in particular and they rely on peoples' ignorance to get the consent to look around. A good rule of thumb when asked for consent to search is to tell the officer: "Officer, I don't have anything to hide, but I don't want you pawing through my stuff."

WHAT IF THEY COME IN ANYWAY?

If an officer of any type enters your home or car without your consent, there are a couple of practical things you should do:

1) Remain calm and courteous, but challenge the officer's right and authority to enter your property by asking why he is entering with out your consent. Even ask the officer to leave, but do it politely;
2) If an officer requests permission to search your person, your vehicle or your home, you should say, "No sir; please get a warrant.";
3) Document every aspect of any incident that you believe constitutes illegal conduct or discourteous, unprofessional or abusive conduct on the part of a peace officer by writing a letter or filing a formal complaint. Include the identity of each person who witnessed the incident, as well as their own handwritten account, if possible; and,
4) Consult a reputable attorney as soon as possible to discuss the officer's actions.

CHAPTER FOUR
Crime and Punishment
CLASSIFICATION OF CRIMES AND OFFENSES

MISDEMEANORS	PUNISHMENT RANGE
Class A	Up to 1 year in County Jail and/or up to $4,000.00 fine.
Class B	Up to 6 months in County Jail and/or up to $2,000.00 fine.
Class C	No Jail; fine up to $500.00.

FELONIES	PUNISHMENT RANGE
Capitol Felony	Life in Prison without parole OR Death Penalty
First Degree	Life in Prison OR 5-99 Years in Prison and/or up to $10,000.00
Second Degree	2-20 Years in Prison and/or up to $10,000.00 fine.
Third Degree	2-10 Years in Prison and/or up to $10,000.00 fine.
State Jail Felony	180 days-2 Years in State jail and/or up to $10,000 fine.

NOTE: Each of the above punishment ranges does not reflect the possibility for Probation or Deferred Adjudication, nor does it reflect enhanced punishments for persons who have prior convictions for various offenses. This chart is intended as a basic reference to certain classification of offenses.

PROBATION

Now referred to as Community Supervision, probation is generally available for those who have a limited or no criminal history and has numerous variations depending on the offense and the individual. Community Supervision is available for all misdemeanor offenses and most felonies whose sentence is ten years or less. Basically, a person placed on Community Supervision agrees to abide by all the conditions the judge sets for the duration of the term of supervision. Any violation can result in revocation or adjudication, which

The Student Body of Law

allows the judge to sentence the probationer to up to the maximum punishment in jail.

It is important to remember that anyone who pleads guilty and receives Community Supervision has waived or given-up the vast majority of his/her rights and protections under the law and is now at the mercy of the Judge.

DEFERRED ADJUDICATION

There is one basic difference between Probation and Deferred Adjudication. Deferred Adjudication ultimately results in the charged offense being dismissed once the individual satisfactorily completes the term of supervision. It is not erased from the records, but the records do reflect that it was dismissed. Therefore, if it was a felony offense, he/she has not been convicted of a felony and retains certain civil rights upon the completion of his/her term of supervision. Probation does not confer this benefit upon the probationer.

THE BAGGAGE OF CONVICTION

Conviction of a crime, particularly a felony, carries with it some serious baggage. Once a person has been convicted of a felony, they lose the right to vote and/or own and use a firearm. Drug convictions can prevent you from receiving financial aid, scholarships, grants, and educational loans. Certain government benefits will not be available and a felony conviction may affect your ability to gain state licenses, such as a license to practice law, CPA, Aviation, and Real Estate. A felony conviction can even adversely affect where you are able to work and live.

Even a misdemeanor conviction can have adverse effects. The most serious are those dealing with theft convictions, but more serious are those associated with felonies. A recent development concerns sex offender registration with the State of Texas and local police agencies. Registration requirements are strict, and if a person who is required to register fails to do so, he or she may be subject to additional felony charges for the failure to comply with the registration requirements. This sort of registration is associated with numerous sex-related convictions and may require registration as a sex offender for the duration of that person's lifetime.

Lastly, the war on drugs has possible grave consequences for students.

Legislation is in effect that disqualifies students from receiving federal student loans if they have any kind of drug conviction. Even a small marijuana possession may disqualify an applicant for federal student loans.

SPEEDING AND OTHER MINOR INFRACTIONS

A speeding ticket and many other minor law infractions are Class C Misdemeanor offenses, which means that you cannot be put in jail if convicted, only fined. You can, however, be arrested for Class C offenses, but are usually only issued a ticket. If you refuse to sign the ticket, the police officer has no choice but to arrest you to make sure you appear in front of a judge on the ticket. Your signature is your promise to appear in court on or before the date on the ticket.

There are many other Class C Misdemeanor violations, such as trespassing, other traffic violations, assault by offensive speech and/or contact, hot checks under $50, certain alcohol violations, noise and nuisance violations, disorderly conduct, and other minor infractions. The most important thing is to take care of it. If you don't take care of it or you fail to appear, a warrant will be issued and the next time you are stopped, you will most likely be arrested and have to make a bond, which is usually the amount equal to the maximum fine of the ticket and a "warrant fee". If you let it go to warrant, you will be stopped and arrested at the most inconvenient time possible, like right before an exam or God forbid, when you really don't want the cop to search your car, which they always do when someone is arrested. You wouldn't believe how many more serious offenses are filed after a search when someone is arrested for warrants. You can't contest the search, because the warrant basically gives the cops the right to search for just about anything.

Class C Misdemeanors usually don't carry too much baggage, unless they are thefts or offenses involving alcohol. These types of offenses usually have habitual violator enhancements that allow the prosecution to elevate the level of offense for repeated violations, as well as Class C violations that are "crimes of moral turpitude." Repeated speeding or moving offenses will be covered later in the Speeding Tickets & Others section.

CRIMES OF MORAL TURPITUDE

A crime of moral turpitude is generally a crime of dishonesty, baseness, or vileness. The crime of moral turpitude is one demonstrating depravity in the private and social duties, which a person owes to another and society at large,

The Student Body of Law

contrary to what is accepted and customary.

A conviction for a crime of moral turpitude may affect or even prevent employment opportunities later in life. A person convicted of a crime of moral turpitude should expect barriers to licensing and/or employment in professions such as banking, attorney, Certified Public Accountant, Securities Broker, and any job requiring that the person be bondable and/or act as a fiduciary. Examples of these types of offenses are:

Any offense against a person with intent to harm;
Theft, fraud or forgery;
Habitual drunkenness or drunk driving;
Illegal gambling;
Prostitution;
Polygamy (marriage to more than one person at the same time);
Any offense that involves perjury or false statements; and
Offenses against a person because of race, religion, national origin, political opinion or social group.

SEX CRIMES & SEX OFFENDER REGISTRATION

The most punitive and long-reaching conviction that carries the biggest and worst set of baggage is a conviction or adjudication of a "sex crime". That's right, commit any crime that is a "reportable conviction or adjudication" and you will have to register as a "sex offender". Our society has placed a greater emphasis on keeping a close watch on sex offenders, with probably very good reason. The U. S. Congress has enacted the Sexually Violent Offender Registration Act and all fifty states have followed suit by enacting various laws requiring convicted sex offender registration of some form or fashion. The Texas Sex Offender Registration Law requires registration for crimes that occurred all the way back to 1970.

That's right, commit any crime that is a "reportable conviction or adjudication" and you will have to register as a "sex offender."

WHAT IS A "SEX CRIME"?

A sex crime in Texas is any of the following offenses: Indecency With a Child (by sexual contact); Sexual Assault; Aggravated Sexual Assault; Aggravated

Kidnapping with intent to sexually abuse; Burglary with intent to commit sexual assault; Indecency with a Child (by exposure) with a prior reportable sex offense conviction; Attempt/Conspiracy/Solicitation or commission of Unlawful Restraint/Kidnapping/Aggravated Kidnapping of a child with a prior reportable sex offence conviction. All of these are also considered "sexually violent offenses". Other reportable sex crimes are: Prohibited Sexual Conduct; Compelling Prostitution; Sexual Performance By a Child; Possession or promotion of child pornography; Attempted Sexual Assault; and, a 2nd conviction for Indecent Exposure.

COLLEGE & UNIVERSITY NOTIFICATION

Anyone that works at or attends college that has a "reportable conviction or adjudication" must register with campus security or the local municipal or county law enforcement agency where the college is located if there is no campus security authority, not later than the seventh day after the date on which the person begins to work or attend school. If terminated, suspended, or otherwise leaving school or employment on campus, the registrant must notify the authorities within seven days of departure.

HOW LONG DOES A SEX OFFENDER HAVE TO REGISTER?
LIFETIME REGISTRATION

A person convicted of a "sexually violent" crime, which is listed above, requires registration annually for their entire life.

Joe's "frisky" performance with his girlfriend in the park, where the local school kids get a good peak of their sexual talents, not to mention their "privates" in our fact pattern in SEXUAL CURIOSITY, PRECOCIOUSNESS & THE PUBLIC, doesn't seem to sound like a very serious case, but be careful. Let's say Joe simply pleads guilty and pays a small fine. The real problem is that Joe fails to understand exactly what it is that he pled guilty to. It is not out of the realm of possibility that if charged and convicted of Indecency with a Child, a conviction or being placed on Deferred Adjudication will force both of them to register as sex offenders. Usually such a situation like Joe's is more likely that not charged, if at all, as Indecent Exposure, which does not require registration. But hold on a minute, this too can carry some lingering affects, because if either Joe or his girlfriend are EVER convicted again for Indecent Exposure, sex offender registration becomes a reality.

The Student Body of Law

LIMITED TERM REGISTRATION

For all other "reportable convictions" that are not "sexually violent" offenses, registration is for ten years after being discharged from probation supervision or release from prison. These "non-sexually violent" crimes are: Prohibited Sexual Conduct; Compelling Prostitution; Sexual Performance By a Child; Possession or promotion of child pornography; Attempted Sexual Assault; or, a second conviction for Indecent Exposure.

Joe and the guys are off to New Orleans for Mardi Gras. While there, they encounter the time-honored tradition of "bead baiting". For those who are uninitiated, some of the ladies who attend Mardi Gras will expose certain parts of their body for the really good beads. Generally speaking, the authorities turn their heads unless it gets really out of hand. Joe decides that he'll get into the action and exposes himself in exchange for some beads. By the way, the New Orleans cops consider this "getting out of hand", even during Mardi Gras. As he unzips and whips it out, the cops crack him in the head with their flashlight and drag him off to jail for indecent exposure. Because of his earlier problem in the park with his girlfriend and his cavalier attitude in pleading guilty, this is his second offense. If convicted, he becomes a registered sex offender. See, GIRLS GONE WILD section of Chapter Six for more of Joe's exploits in this area.

IT'S A CRIME NOT TO REGISTER

If required to register as a sex offender, non-compliance with the registration law are either State Jail or Third Degree Felonies, depending on the offense requiring registration. There are quite a lot of technical requirements under the registration statute and all requirements must be strictly followed, otherwise a registrant may be prosecuted for a completely separate crime.

WHAT ELSE DO CONVICTED SEX OFFENDERS HAVE TO DO?

Just in case you weren't totally convinced that registering as a sex offender is not an incredibly humiliating and demeaning thing to do, a conviction has the potential to send someone to prison for a very long time. Over and above the threat of prison, there are other possible requirements, conditions, and implications that may be imposed on or endured by convicted sex offenders. Anyone who is a registered sex offender may have the following information published or otherwise made public: address, photograph, date of birth, social security number and driver's license number. There is usually some kind of neighborhood alert/notifications by neighborhood associations and activists, as well as listings of this information in databases available to the public.

Over and above these, certain things may come along with probation. A judge granting community supervision to a defendant required to register as a sex offender under Chapter 62 shall require that the defendant, as a condition of community supervision: 1) submit a blood sample or other specimen to the DPS to create a DNA record for a DNA database; 2) submit to treatment, specialized supervision, or rehabilitation according to offense-specific standards of practice adopted by the Council on Sex Offender Treatment and pay all or part of the reasonable and necessary costs of the treatment, supervision, or rehabilitation.

If the victim of the sex crime was a child, the judge will establish a "child safety zone" by ordering the "sex offender" 1) from supervising or participating in any program that includes participants that are seventeen or younger, such as athletic, civic, or cultural activities; or 2) from going in, on, or within 1,000 feet of a premises where children commonly gather, including a school, day-care facility, playground, public or private youth center, public swimming pool, or video arcade facility; and 3) to attend psychological counseling sessions. These "child safety zone" requirements may be lifted by the Court only if: 1) the sex offender is a student at a primary or secondary school; 2) it interferes with the ability of the person to attend school or hold a job and consequently constitutes an undue hardship for the defendant; or 3) is broader than is necessary to protect the public, given the nature and circumstances of the offense.

The term of probation may even be extended by the Court for ten more years if the judge determines that the probationer has not sufficiently demonstrated a commitment to avoid future criminal behavior and that the release of the defendant from supervision would endanger the public. The judge may extend the period of supervision for a period not to exceed ten additional years.

These are not all of the possible terms and conditions available and creative judges have been known to require other conditions, such as posting a sign on the person's front door that alerts the community that they are a sex offender, or personally notify the residences of their neighborhood just to name a couple. Generally speaking, a judge may not require a defendant to undergo an orchiectomy, which is surgical testicular removal or as a condition of community supervision.

The Student Body of Law

YOUR RECORD
Remember that night you were arrested late one night outside the What-a-burger for what was it? Public Intoxication, Assault, MIP. You don't even really remember what happened to the case. Who knows if it may be on your record?. Hell, what is a record these days?

CRIMINAL RECORDS
In the old days before computers, a person's record referred to their rap sheet. The records relating to convictions and arrests were not readily accessible to the public due to the nature of physical documentary record keeping. A background check was an extremely time-intensive search of individual county and state records to piece together a person's record. It is no longer that difficult these days. If you have been arrested and charged with a crime, records relating to your arrest and identifying information are entered throughout the criminal justice system in huge computer databases.

Imagine the flow of information: the arresting agency, for example, Houston Police Department, enters your name into their computers. Upon arriving at the jail, the record of your arrest is entered into the jail records; photographs and fingerprints are taken and sent to the Texas Department of Public Safety, as well as the AFIS System of digitized fingerprint analysis and is placed in a national database where a file with your name is opened and those items are recorded and stored. DPS can also forward these records to federal law enforcement agencies. If you were interviewed by Harris County Pre-Trial Services for release on personal bond, your information will be entered in their computer. The local County and District Clerk, as well as the District Attorney's Office will both open files and enter your information into their computers. If the arrest involved a driver's license suspension, whether ultimately suspended or not, Texas DPS will make those notations in your Driving Record. Not only is the traditional paper trail growing, the digital trail grows. Criminal records are maintained by the Texas Department of Public Safety in the Texas Crime Information Computer (TCIC) and the Federal Bureau of Investigations in its National Crime Information Computer (NCIC). These agencies' record databases are not open to the public, but law enforcement and prosecutorial offices can check these records any time they like. The general public has full access to files in all District and County Clerk's Offices in the State of Texas, but not these.

Many people have the misconception that if their case was dismissed, the records no longer exist. If you have been arrested and charged with a crime, getting the case dismissed does not mean that the records disappear. Granted, a criminal record does not exist, but any and all entities that made a record of your arrest and/or prosecution retain those records, unless a court orders the destruction of those records.

The County or District Clerk's Office, or the Municipal Court where you were charged has a file concerning the incident, which is public information. That means future employers, credit services, banks, or any other person or entity that wants to search your past records can do so. The accessibility to these records becomes easier as more and more of these records are computerized. Anyone can discover prior criminal conduct by simply searching for your name at the county courthouse or municipal court or on-line if they know where to search. More and more companies use these background searches as screening tools of potential employees. The record of the arrest, the offense report, fingerprints, case disposition, etc… are still around unless you act to expunge those records.

Many people have the misconception that if their case was dismissed, the records no longer exist.

DO I HAVE A CRIMINAL RECORD?

If you think you may have any arrest or conviction or just want to make sure, you might want to check out your own criminal history to see what is going to come up before someone else sees it. You can do this by mail or in person from the Texas Department of Public Safety who maintains all criminal records for Texas. An individual or their authorized representative has access to and may receive a copy of their Criminal History Record Information (CHRI). This policy is in compliance with Texas Government Code section 552.023. A written request for the CHRI must be submitted along with:

1. Printed name of the individual. Include any other names used. (Order of names: LAST, MIDDLE, FIRST);
2. Sex;
3. Race;
4. Date of Birth: (Month / Day / Year);

The Student Body of Law

5. A complete and legible set of fingerprints on a DPS approved fingerprint card taken by a law enforcement officer. Most local police and sheriff's departments will provide this service and may charge a fee, often $5. However, it is the responsibility of the individual to mail or bring the completed card to Austin, along with the other necessary information. If you go to DPS in Austin, they will fingerprint you and run the CHRI all for $15 and it takes between 2-4 hours;
6. Social Security Number;
7. Return address and phone number of the individual or authorized representative;
8. Cash, check or U.S. money order for $15.00 per each fingerprint card.
Mail the written request and the fingerprint card with payment to:
Texas Department of Public Safety
Crime Records Service
P.O. Box 15999
Austin, Texas 78761-5999
Attention: Correspondence Supervisor

If a criminal history record is found, it along with the original fingerprint card will be returned, if no record is found a notation of such will be made on the fingerprint card and it will be returned with a notation indicating no criminal record.

CLEANING-UP YOUR RECORD - EXPUNCTION

The only way that records of arrest and prosecution can be removed is under a process known as expunction, whereby an individual, through his/her attorney, files a civil law suit against all departments and entities that maintain those records to expunge or destroy the records. Generally, if a misdemeanor has been dismissed or acquitted by the judge or a jury, then expunction is available. If a felony has been dismissed before being presented to a Grand Jury, acquitted by a judge or a jury, or dismissed and the statute of limitations has run, then an expunction is available. If the case was presented to the Grand Jury based upon mistake, false information, or other such situation, then expunction may also be available. One last requirement is that the person seeking expunction has not been convicted of a felony in the five years preceding the date of the arrest.

In order to have your records expunged, a petition for expunction must be drafted and filed in the District Court of the county where you were arrested; all parties retaining records must be named and served; and the petition must be presented to the Court for ruling. Once the Court determines that you qualify under the statute, the Court orders that any agency or entity named that has in their possession any record of your arrest or prosecution is ordered to destroy the entire record, fingerprints, booking photo, arrest report, including the DPS records. It is as if the arrest never occurred.

LEGAL EFFECT OF EXPUNCTION

1) the release, dissemination, or use of the expunged records and files for any purpose is prohibited; 2) you may deny the occurrence of the arrest and the existence of the expunction order, with the exception of the following; 3) you or any other person, when questioned under oath in a criminal proceeding about an arrest for which the records have been expunged, may state only that the matter in question has been expunged. (See Texas Code of Criminal Procedure, Art. 55.03). As the laws are continually amended, there is some debate and legal wrangling over these records and whether or not law enforcement and/or government can retain the records for their own use. Notwithstanding the continuing concerns regarding government's overreaching or improper uses of these records, the most important aspect is the removal of these records from public view and the right to deny their occurrence.

NON-DISCLOSURE OF RECORDS & DEFERRED ADJUDICATION

Unfortunately, many people are erroneously told that if they agree to

The Student Body of Law

a term of Deferred Adjudication, it will result in no criminal record and the case is dismissed after you successfully serve the probation period. This is partially correct. When the case is dismissed, the records of the arrest, prosecution, and deferred adjudication remain for all to see. If you are placed on court ordered supervision, you are not entitled to have your records expunged. Successfully completing a term of deferred adjudication does not result in a conviction, but your criminal history will always show that you were arrested, charged, and the case was dismissed. A deferred adjudication that qualifies under certain legal guidelines passed by the Texas Legislature in 2003 can now be sealed from public dissemination. Like expunction, this too requires petitioning the court of supervision, presentation to the court, and other legal requirements, but may be available to further protect you from prying eyes.

A Petition for Non-Disclosure may be filed upon the dismissal/discharge in most Misdemeanor cases, except Misdemeanors involving: Kidnapping; Unlawful Restraint; Sexual Offenses; Assaultive Offenses; Offenses Against the Family; Disorderly Conduct & Related Offenses; & Weapons Violations, in which case one must wait five years after dismissal/discharge to file a petition; and, ten years following discharge/dismissal in all qualified felonies.

There are other limitations such as: (1) anyone who has been convicted or placed on Deferred Adjudication for any offense (except Transportation Code violations punishable by fine only) during the applicable time periods above do not qualify; and (2) anyone ever convicted or placed on Deferred Adjudication for any offense requiring Sex Offender Registration; aggravated kidnapping; murder; capital murder; injury to child, elderly or disabled; abandoning or endangering child; violation of magistrates protective order; stalking; any offense involving "Family Violence" (Sec. 71.004 FAM Code definition).

Other limitations may also arise, as the Texas Legislature continues to tinker with this statute and will probably continue to do so. If you are interested in exploring the possibility or are worried about a record of arrest, charge, or conviction, consult with a reputable attorney for more particular advice.

JUVENILE RECORDS

Everyone seems to think that once you turn eighteen your record is somehow wiped clean and you start over. This is not the case. Generally speaking, convictions while a minor cannot be used to enhance punishment of adult offenses, however in some instances they can be considered at punishment, and any offense that relates to alcohol and/or tobacco and drugs remains viable and can be used to elevate the seriousness of subsequent offenses.

EXPUNCTION OF JUVENILE RECORDS

If you were convicted of only one minor/alcohol offense under the Texas Alcohol & Beverage Code, once you turn twenty-one, you may apply to the court in which you were convicted to have the conviction expunged. Otherwise there is no mechanism for expunging these records.

SEALING JUVENILE RECORDS

Once the records are sealed, information relating to the arrest, detention, prosecution, and conviction are physically sealed and/or destroyed. If these records are sealed then people do start adulthood with a clean record and this authorizes the person to state that they have never been convicted. Any juvenile charge that results in a finding of Not Guilty automatically qualifies it to be sealed and the court is under a duty to immediately order the sealing of all files and records relating to the case.

Generally speaking, juvenile records may be sealed if:

1. Two years have elapsed since final discharge of the person or since the last official action in the person's case if there was no adjudication; and

2. The person has not been convicted of a felony or a misdemeanor involving moral turpitude or found to have engaged in delinquent conduct or conduct indicating a need for supervision and no proceeding is pending seeking conviction or adjudication during those two years.

Once a person reaches the age of twenty-one, a person may petition the court to order the sealing of records concerning a juvenile felony if:

1. The person was not "certified" as an adult;

2. The records have not been used as evidence in the punishment phase of a criminal proceeding under Article 37.07, Code of Texas Criminal Procedure; and,

3. The person has not been convicted of a felony after becoming age seventeen.

The Student Body of Law

Some juvenile criminal offenses that resulted in a determinate sentence are not eligible for sealing such as: murder, capital murder, manslaughter, aggravated kidnapping, sexual assault, aggravated sexual assault, aggravated assault, injury to a child/elderly/disabled person, arson, indecency with a child, and engaging in habitual felony conduct.

"IT WASN'T ME, IT WAS HIM"

It's late and the bars have closed. No place will sell you beer, but you and your buddies aren't quite ready to call it a night. You all jokingly talk about stealing some beer from the local convenience store, but you all laugh and forget about it. Your buddy, Joe, asks you to stop at the store so he can buy some cigarettes. You stop and wait for him to go in. All of a sudden, Joe runs out of the store with two cases of beer under his arms, jumps in the car yelling, "go, go, go!!!" and you speed off. Although you are plenty pissed off at your friend, you get over it as you all finish off the case of beer he snagged from the store. The next day a knock at the door reveals a police officer and BANG, you are arrested for Theft. How can that be if you really didn't do anything but drive off after Joe had already stolen the beer?

PARTIES TO A CRIME

You may be criminally responsible for any offense committed by another if you promote or assist the commission of the offense, by soliciting, encouraging, directing, aiding, or attempt to aid the other person in committing the offense, or if you have a legal duty to prevent the commission of the offense and act, but instead you and fail to make a reasonable effort to prevent commission of the offense; or you cause someone to commit a crime, without them actually realizing it.

In the situation above, you aided in the commission and flight by driving the getaway car.

You have probably seen on the news where two guys go into a store to rob the place and one of them shoots the clerk. Both robbers will most likely be charged with the Capital Murder of the clerk, because it is reasonably foreseeable that in the course of a robbery someone may get hurt or even killed, even if the other guy didn't know the shooter had a gun.

CONSPIRACY

One boring Friday night, you and some of the guys hatch a plan to steal some beer from the local country club. One of you worked there for a while and you know that they keep some beer and liquor in a storage locker. You all plan the caper and each of you has a role to play. One of you will drive; one is gonna get out and cut the lock and the other two will go in and get the booze and load it in the trunk. BANG a conspiracy is born; conspiracy to commit the offense of Burglary of a Building.

All that needs to happen to complete the crime is one of you to do anything in furtherance of the agreement. All of you getting in the car with the tools to break the lock and starting out will probably do it, even if you get to the country club and you decide that this is really not such a good idea.

A conspiracy is simply an agreement between two or more people to engage in conduct that would constitute an offense and one or more of them perform an overt act in pursuance of the agreement. This, in and of itself, is a crime, whether or not the actual crime is ultimately committed or not and is one category lower than the most serious felony that is the object of the conspiracy, and if the most serious felony that is the object of the conspiracy is a State Jail felony, the offense is a Class A misdemeanor. If, in the attempt to carry out a conspiracy to commit one felony, another felony is committed by one of the conspirators, all conspirators are guilty of the felony actually committed, though having no intent to commit it, if the offense was committed in furtherance of the unlawful purpose and was one that should have been anticipated as a result of the carrying out of the conspiracy. Conspiracy is rarely prosecuted in Texas state courts. The next section is the more popular offense prosecuted in these types of situation.

ORGANIZED CRIMINAL ACTIVITY

This is similar to a conspiracy in that a person commits an offense if he establishes, maintains, or participates in a combination or in the profits of a combination or as a member of a criminal street gang, he commits or conspires to commit one or more of the specific crimes listed under this section of the penal code, which are numerous.

Once involved in an organized criminal activity, the only way out is a voluntary and complete renunciation of his criminal objective by withdrawing from the combination before commission of an offense listed and take further affirmative action that prevents the commission of the offense.

The Student Body of Law

"I DIDN'T REALLY DO ANYTHING" ATTEMPTED CRIMES

The offense of Criminal Attempt is committed if, with specific intent to commit an offense, the person does an act amounting to more than mere preparation that tends, but fails, to effect the commission of the offense intended. It is no defense to prosecution for criminal attempt that the offense attempted was not actually committed. An attempted offense is one category lower than the offense attempted.

Never discuss the facts of the arrest or charge with anyone except your attorney and never over the jail phone.

ARREST & BAIL

You find yourself being asked to place your hands behind your back and are being taken into custody; you are under arrest; you are placed in the back seat of a patrol car and BANG, you're going to jail. Hopefully, you did not skip right to this section, but first read the section regarding GENERAL ADVICE CONCERNING THE POLICE "DEALING WITH THE LOCAL CONSTABULARY" A PRIMER IN MANNERS, CUSTOM AND DECORUM WHEN "DEALING WITH THE COPS". AND YOUR CONSTITUTIONAL RIGHTS, including your right to remain silent.

The U.S Constitution, the Texas Constitution, and the Texas Code of Criminal Procedure recognize the right to be released on reasonable bond. Upon arrest, the citizen is initially taken to the jail of the arresting agency and must, without unnecessary delay, be taken before a magistrate. All citizens arrested, if not released by the arresting agency, are eventually booked into jail, usually the local county jail and are taken before a magistrate. At that appearance, the magistrate must inform the accused of his constitutional rights and determine whether probable cause exists for the arrest and whether a bond should be set. This procedure usually occurs within twenty-four hours of the arrest. Do not plead guilty to the charge in front of the magistrate unless you are completely certain that is what you want to do, because it will result in a conviction and remain on your criminal record.

You will normally be given an opportunity to make a phone call, but again, this is reality and not TV, and you don't get one phone call by right. Remain courteous throughout. Being rude and obnoxious will not help in your defense.

If and when you do get access to a phone, call someone you know will answer and accept a collect call, because it seems like all calls from the jail are collect. Your roommate answers and you tell him quickly and calmly that he needs to find this book and read about bail, then scrape together some money and get you out or call your parents. Never discuss the facts of the arrest or charge with anyone except your attorney and never over the jail phone. These phones are regularly monitored and recorded, as are conversations in the cells and rooms of the jail.

In most counties, bonds are determined based upon a "bond schedule" that has been approved by the judges currently presiding, which sets a standard bail amount for the various degrees of crimes charged. Under certain circumstances, bond is denied to an accused. A judge may set bail, or reduce or even raise the bail amount depending on the circumstances. In order to be released on bond, a citizen can achieve release three different ways:

1) Post a cash bond in the full amount of the bond. If the person on bond appears as directed, once the case has been resolved, the cash bond will be returned, usually within six to twelve weeks;

2) Hire a professional bondsman to post the bail for you. A professional bondsman will charge a fee for his service, usually anywhere between five to twenty percent of the bond, depending on the circumstances and collateral. The bondsman is licensed and has an agreement with the county holding the citizen to guarantee the appearance of the citizen at all court ordered appearances; otherwise, the bond is forfeited and the bondsman is responsible for the entire amount of the bond; or,

3) Most counties in Texas have a Pretrial Service Agency that administers the pretrial release of accused citizens. Based upon an interview and the recommendations of the Pretrial Agency, the judge will decide whether or not to grant a pretrial bond for a particular defendant. Release in this manner is far less expensive for the accused. However, the Pretrial Services Agency will most likely require more effort and conditions than a bonding company.

Once your roommate has scurried around all morning trying to spring you from the slammer, you are finally released on bond. First things first, go home and take a shower, second, take your roommate out to breakfast, no matter how awful an experience your night in the slammer was, his was equal-

The Student Body of Law

ly frustrating and unpleasant dealing with the bureaucracy of the authorities that didn't really want to let you out.

In the worst case scenario, for some reason your roommate couldn't get you out because your case said "no bond". A "no bond" designation means that the citizen is not afforded the right to a reasonable bond and will not be released if:

1) The citizen is currently on probation or on bond for a felony;
2) The citizen is charged with a crime of violence;
3) The citizen has previously been sentenced to prison two or more times; or
4) The citizen has been arrested pursuant to a "blue warrant" (violation of parole).

Unless one of these situations apply, don't freak out. A "no bond" designation does not always mean that the person will not get a bond set, but you will most-likely have to wait until you are taken before a judge and your attorney should approach the judge to request that reasonable bond be set.

I THINK I HAVE A WARRANT

You pick-up your date one Friday night; it's the third date and you are expecting some action later in the evening. On the way to the party, you roll through a stop sign and after the cop runs your license, he asks you to step out of the car. BANG, you have a warrant. The speeding ticket you got last spring break had escaped your memory and went to warrant. Instead of real funky love action after the party, you get to spend the night with all the other losers in the holdover cell.

Like we talked about earlier, warrants usually come back to bite you at a really inconvenient time. If you think you have a warrant out for your arrest, contact the local law enforcement agencies that may have a record of your warrant and ask if they would run your identifying information to confirm the warrant. Don't worry, they are not going to trace your call and come right out to arrest you, unless of course you are really wanted, they actually want you to clear the warrant and will usually give you whatever information you need to clear it, if not call a lawyer or bondsman. If you have a warrant, you have four basic choices:

1. Wait until a law enforcement officer takes you to jail;
2. Turn yourself in to the local jail;

3. Pay the full amount of the bond (i.e. cash bond); or
4. Post a bond with a bail bond agency.

Collect up your money and go make the bond. Don't take the risk of losing your job or being embarrassed in front of your family, friends, co-workers, or even your class.

ANATOMY OF A TRIAL

Voir Dire: French for "to speak the truth", otherwise known as jury selection. The jury panel is questioned by the judge and the lawyers for all parties and each side gets to strike a certain number for any reason they want. The first six or twelve eligible people left, depending on the jury's size, are the jury.

Opening Statements: Attorneys for each side are allowed to address the jury and may explain the case, discuss the evidence and facts they intend or believe will be presented, and detail the issues the jury will ultimately be asked to decide. It is usually a pretty broad overview of each side's case and sets the stage for what's ahead. The State, or Plaintiff, always has the option of going first.

Presentation of Evidence: Testimony of witnesses and exhibits introduced are all evidence. Any exhibits introduced are available to the jury during their deliberations. The State presents its evidence in its "case in chief" and the Defense may present evidence or witnesses after the State has rested. The Defense does not have to present any evidence or witnesses and may rest immediately after the State, if they choose. Once a witness has been called to testify by one side and questioned, the other side gets to cross-examine the witness.

Testimony: Either party may subpoena witnesses to testify, however the State cannot call the Defendant to testify. The decision to testify is solely left to the Defense and a Defendant's election not to testify cannot be considered by the jury for any reason.

Witnesses: The jury decides the credibility of the witness and can accept or reject all or part of any witness'es testimony for any reason, but they must start each witness at the same level of credibility before they ever say a word.

Objections by the Attorneys: The attorneys are ethically obligated to not only represent their client(s), whether the State, a Plaintiff, or a Defendant, zealously to the best of their abilities, but also to ensure that all the rules of evidence and procedure are followed. Whenever they think these rules are not being followed, they must make an objection on the record.

Rulings by the Judge: The judge decides all questions of law during the trial. The judge also rules on the lawyers' objections, keeps the trial in order, and has wide discretion over the courtroom and those that are either there or have been ordered to appear to do so. The judge may even ask jurors, witnesses, and observers to leave the courtroom to prevent them from hearing arguments or evidence that may or may not be admitted into evidence or just to keep order.

Instruction to the Jury: After all evidence has been presented, the judge will give the jury the Charge of the Court. This includes the law relating to the specific case the jury heard and the question(s) the jury must answer.

Closing Arguments: Lawyers for each side are allowed to summarize the evidence to try to persuade the jury to accept their view of the case. It is not evidence, just the lawyer's view of the evidence.

Jury Deliberations and Decision: After closing arguments, the jury is sent to deliberate and can only consider the evidence admitted and testimony they heard at trial. The jury will decide how they will answer the questions given to them in the Charge of the Court and then reach a verdict by answering these questions.

THE OTHER SIDE – THE COMPLAINING WITNESS

We have been talking about the accused quite a lot and it is just as important that any Citizen that feels they have been wronged, has the right to bring that person or entity into court to answer for their actions. In civil matters it's usually a question of money or divorce, but if the Citizen feels that it is criminal act, they can swear out complaints and aid the State in charging and prosecuting the case.

FILING CHARGES

Contact the local law enforcement office and make a formal report and/or complaint, but do not try to use the system as leverage or intimidation. Whenever you report a crime, be accurate and truthful at all times, otherwise you may subject *yourself* to criminal prosecution.

VICTIM'S RIGHTS

There are specific rights associated with those who have been victims of crime. If you have been the victim of sexual assault, kidnapping, or aggravated robbery, or if you have suffered bodily injury as the result of another's crime, or if you are the close relative or guardian of a deceased victim, you have the right to:

1. be protected from harm or threats;
2. information about the defendant's right to bail and to have your safety considered in the setting of bail;
3. information about court proceedings, if you so request, and to be present at all public proceedings subject to the approval of the judge;
4. information about stages in the criminal justice system in general including criminal investigations, trials, plea bargaining, appeals, and parole;
5. provide information to the probation department concerning the impact of the crime for inclusion in the pre-sentence investigation report to the judge, and to complete a Victim Impact Statement;
6. information regarding compensation to crime victims under the Crime Victims' Compensation Act, payment for a medical examination for a victim of sexual assault and referral to available social service agencies that may offer additional assistance;
7. notification, if requested, of any parole proceedings regarding the defendant, and the right to participate in those proceedings;
8. a waiting area in the courthouse separate from the defendant and his or her family and witnesses, or if a separate area is not possible, to have safeguards to insure minimal contact;
9. prompt return of property held by law enforcement or the attorney for the state after the property is not longer needed as evidence;
10. notification to your employer by the prosecuting attorney, if you must be absent from work in order to be in court or to otherwise cooperate in the case.

PROTECTIVE ORDERS

A Citizen may request the County or District Attorney's Office to protect family members and individuals involved in a dating relationship at no cost. The citizen will have to fill out and execute a sworn affidavit that sets out the facts supporting that violence has occurred in the past and is likely to occur in the future. Once a complaint is filed and the affidavit is received, an

The Student Body of Law

Application for a Protective Order and Temporary Protective Order will be filed and presented to a District Judge. The judge will review the application and affidavit and if sufficient evidence exists, will sign and enter the Temporary Protective Order and set a hearing within fourteen days. The Respondent will then be served and notified to be at the hearing. Both parties normally appear at the hearing, with a permanent Protective Order being entered. The Protective Order can be up to two years and can require alcohol, drug, and anger counseling.

The court may also prohibit or order either party to or not do any number of things involving counseling, places they cannot go, people they cannot contact or see, possession of property, including forbidding them access to their own children and homes.

CHAPTER FIVE
Adult vs. 21

You have made it out of high school and have embarked on the pursuit of a college education. Good for you and keep at it. This also means that for the vast majority reading this, you have also just moved off to school and out from under the loving, but watchful, eye of your parental unit(s). One other assumption is that you are probably seventeen to eighteen years old. Now, I certainly understand that you see yourself as an adult and full well can act as such. Unfortunately, our society over the past twenty or so years has become increasingly of the opinion that seventeen, and even eighteen, years of age does not necessarily confer upon you much of the legal privileges accorded a citizen, but have remained resolute that eighteen means that you have become saddled with the full responsibilities and liabilities heaped upon us, but without the fun. It ain't fair but that's the way it is.

17 & 18

Once you turn eighteen years old, you are an adult and are expected to act accordingly. According to the criminal laws in Texas, you are an adult upon turning seventeen and you can be prosecuted as an adult and are no longer considered a juvenile. The old myth that any juvenile criminal record(s) are either sealed or destroyed is no longer true, if it ever was. It is true that any criminal convictions cannot be used to enhance future adult punishments, however it can be taken into consideration when a judge or jury is determining an appropriate sentence. If you have not turned eighteen yet, well you may still have some form of curfew, so check with the local authorities so you know exactly what it is.

VOTING

The most important right that vests once you are eighteen, is the right to vote. Take this new right to heart and vote every opportunity you can. Sadly,

The Student Body of Law

as a group the eighteen to twenty-four year olds vote less than any other group. So if all these laws targeted at you don't motivate you to educate yourself a little about your elected representatives and vote for those who will represent your interests, you will probably continue to see more and more restrictions on your freedoms.

If you attend college away from home and are registered to vote at your parents' address, you have several voting options. You may register to vote at your new college residence or keep your voter registration current at your parents' address. You decide where you reside for voting purposes, but you cannot register in both locations. If you keep your voter registration at your parents' address and will not be home during the early voting period or on Election Day, you can request that a ballot by mail be sent to you at your college address.

I suggest that you register to vote in the town in which you are going to school; it's where you spend the most time and where you are most affected by the local government. It's your home. Why shouldn't it reflect the will of the people that live there? Elections will most always occur during the semester and you will be spending the majority of your time there, so why not have a say in what is happening both locally and otherwise? Most colleges have political clubs and societies that may interest you and being registered to vote will be an important part of the participation. Who knows? You may even meet a member of the opposite sex that has the same political views as you. Or maybe someone that you can argue with and then go have a beer. Voting impacts almost every aspect of our lives, so get out there and vote. An old college professor of mine always preached: "If you don't vote, you don't have the right to bitch about what your government is doing."

Suffrage, although it sounds bad, is actually a very good thing. It is the right to vote and began way before we embraced the concept in forming the United States. Centuries ago, in the Greek city-states, all freemen were expected to take part in the government of their city, although the freeman population was a minority of the population, there were no "career politicians" as they served as representatives for very short terms on a rotating/lottery-style basis. Ancient Rome incorporated certain voting rights in their government by allowing the common citizens, called plebs, the right to elect tribunes, which would represent them to address unfair or oppressive treatment by the government. Even before Columbus arrived, the Native American Iriquois nation of the northeastern U.S. had embraced their own style of democracy, which employed a citizen-run government and even included women tribe members.

Although these concepts were around, it really wasn't until the 17th & 18th centuries that the idea cemented that the people should actually have some say in the way their government was run by selecting who ran the government. These concepts gathered a little bit of credibility when Western philosophers of the Enlightenment began to debate the idea that self-government is a natural right and the power given to the government is only because those being governed have consented to that power.

The U.S. Constitution originally allowed each individual state to determine its own voter qualifications; but the states' inabilities to incorporate constitutionally valid qualifications resulted in a national call for change. Amendments to the U.S. Constitution were necessary to prohibit states from denying the right to vote based on race or sex, or charging a poll tax in national elections. Literacy tests were also used to keep certain "undesirable" persons from voting. The Civil Rights Act of 1965 put a stop to that by banning such restrictions in any state that had less than fifty percent of the population registered to vote and amendments to the Civil Rights Act ultimately banned state literacy tests outright, also requiring that ballots be printed in languages other than English where there was a substantial portion of the population that was literate in another language.

1970 brought more changes when the U.S. Supreme Court ruled that eighteen year olds had the right to vote in all federal elections (the age limit in most states was twenty-one). The 26th Amendment to the Constitution made this a right in all elections in 1971.

JURY DUTY

Another right you are now vested with is the right to serve on a jury, commonly referred to as "jury duty". Every citizen owes it to his or her country, local government, fellow citizens and to him or herself, to appear for jury service. Many people see jury service as a huge pain, taking them away from their daily lives and responsibilities, but should see it for what it really is: the closest and truest impact you can have on the proper function of our government.

The U.S. and the State of Texas Constitutions guarantee a right to trial by jury for anyone accused of a crime, regardless of his or her race, religion, gender, national origin, or economic status. So important, it was even included

The Student Body of Law

in the Texas Declaration of Independence. Any time the facts of a civil or criminal case are in dispute, the parties have a right to have their case heard by a jury of fair and impartial citizens who will make decisions without bias or prejudice.

The concept of a jury trial is hardly new, dating back to medieval England, but is not a concept that has been adopted by many societies. The vast majority of countries throughout the world consider the idea that we put the power to decide what is against the law, who committed a crime and decide who gets money, child custody, and many other important decisions, in the hands of everyday citizens as an insane way to operate. What those people don't realize is that in the United States the power lies with the people, not the government, and the jury system is just one more way the citizens are vested with the power to make sure that the government is doing what the citizens feel is best for the country and not the other way around.

Obviously, to have a jury trial, you've got to have a jury; and to have a jury, citizens from all walks of life must be called upon to participate; that's where you come into the picture. Because you have received a jury summons, you are now placed in a position of power most people in the world will never experience. You have the opportunity to see the justice system up close and if selected to serve on a jury, will participate in one of this country's most fundamental processes.

Qualifications to be a Juror. A citizen is qualified to sit as a juror if that person:

1) is at least eighteen years of age;
2) is a resident of the county in which you are called to serve;
3) is a United States citizen;
4) is qualified under the constitution and laws to vote in the county in which one is to serve as a juror. (you do not have to be a registered voter to serve);
5) is of sound mind and good moral character;
6) is able to read, write, and understand/speak English;
7) has not served as a petit juror for six days in the preceding six months in a district court or six days in the preceding three months in a county court;
8) has not been convicted of a theft or any felony; and,
9) is not under indictment or other legal accusation for a theft or any felony.

Now that you have a better idea of what jury duty is and who can be a juror, you may be wondering how it is that you are called for jury service. The process for selecting prospective jurors is mandated by state law. If you are a registered voter, have a Texas driver's license or Texas personal identification card, your name is entered in a computer system in the county where you live that randomly selects prospective jurors to serve. In order to try to avoid duplicate names, the Secretary of State combines the names from the voter registration list and the DPS list, the problem is that their software cannot detect duplicates if there is any difference in name or address between the two sources. This means that sometimes, a person may receive more than one jury summons within a short period of time. Don't worry, you won't get called over and over, you are exempted if you have served within the past thirty-six months.

What about my job and school? The law protects your job while you are fulfilling your jury duty. Your employer does not have to pay you, but they can't fire you for fulfilling your duty. This applies to school as well. You may have to make-up the work, but your attendance will be excused with either an excuse from the court or a phone call from the judge personally to the professor or department head, maybe even the dean or president. Judges usually don't like anyone that disrupts their ability to hold court.

What to Wear? If you're heading out for jury duty, you may want to take a book, homework, or other reading material, maybe even your Gameboy. Jury duty involves a certain amount of idle time and waiting, so come prepared to pass the time. Plan to spend the day, and if you're cut loose early, consider it a reward for serving your country. Some courts have dress codes, so dress appropriately. Jury service is serious business, and you should dress accordingly. That doesn't mean a suit, but cutoffs, tank tops, and flip-flops won't cut it either. Be respectful of the courts, their staff and your fellow jurors.

Juror De-Selection. During jury selection, the lawyers are not deciding who they want on the jury, they are deciding who they don't want. Prospective jurors are assigned to smaller groups, may fill out questionnaires and are taken to a courtroom by a bailiff, briefed by the judge and questioned by attorneys. You may be asked questions about your opinions about a variety of issues and subjects. Each side is given a certain number of strikes that they can use on any juror they do not want on the jury. The first six or twelve

The Student Body of Law

(depending on the court) persons on the panel that have not been either excused by the judge because they indicated they couldn't follow the law or are struck by either side are then selected for the jury.

I Can't Serve. As mentioned before, some people see this incredible right as a pain and lots of these same types ask me how they can get out of jury duty. As I have mentioned before, I personally don't think that this is the way to look at it, but since we live a in free society, they, too, are entitled to their opinion, even if it is exactly this type of duty that guarantees their right to that opinion. For these people, I'm going to make them read some more before I tell them the real secrets to getting out of being selected on a jury. Lots of times, people can't serve because they have other things planned that they can't reschedule, if that's the case, contact the district, county, or court clerk listed on the summons to try to re-schedule your service to a time that is more convenient. Most clerks have such procedures in place and are more than happy to try to accommodate your schedule in advance.

Exemptions from Service. There are some exemptions from service, which do not disqualify a citizen, but lets you get out of it, if you qualify and want to. These exemptions are for:

1) Citizens over seventy years of age;
2) Citizens with legal custody of children under ten years old when jury service would leave those children without adequate supervision (this does not apply to those who work outside the home during normal business hours or those whose children are in a daycare facility during the day);
3) Students in private or public high schools or attending an institution of higher education (you must be enrolled and attending classes at the time you are summoned to appear);
4) Citizens associated with the legislative branch as an officer or an employee of the senate, house of representatives, or any department, commission, board, office, or other agency in the legislative branch of state government;
5) Citizens who have appeared as a petit juror in the county during the thirty-sex month period preceding the date he/she is to appear. (this does not apply to those who have served in a city or federal court);
6) Citizens who are primary caretakers of those unable to care for themselves (this does not apply to health care workers); and,

7) Citizens who have a medical condition and submit physician's documentation of such with the sworn Affidavit Form.

There are several common misconceptions regarding exemptions that are NOT reasons for exemption:
1) being the sole owner of a business or commission sales;
2) having an employer who will not pay you for your jury service;
3) travel frequently for business; and,
4) having a lack of transportation

This SUCKS, how do I get out of it? Okay, for those who really don't want to serve on a jury, but don't qualify for the exemption, you will still have to show-up and sit through the jury selection part of jury duty. I hope that this is pure hell for you and it seems like an eternity. I tell jurors all the time that a sure-fire way to get put on a jury is to sit there and say absolutely nothing, because when I go back to review my notes and jury chart, I don't have any reason to strike them. It is usually those prospective jurors that volunteer, raise their hands, and are outspoken about a question asked or issue raised that end up getting struck by one side or the other. Anytime that a juror categorically states that they cannot follow the law, are unable to swear an oath to follow the law or state that they are biased against one side or the other, without even hearing any evidence, these citizens are most always excused for cause by the judge. Be forewarned, this is not some trick to try in the courtroom. Prospective jurors have been held in contempt for their antics and outspoken behavior. If the judge feels you are being obstreperous, disruptive, or disingenuous with the Court, you may be held in contempt and ordered to do something much worse than serve on a jury, like sit in a jail cell, or in one instance, a judge ordered a prospective juror to attend every day of the trial and submit to the judge at the end of each week, a hand written report of the week's developments at trial. The trial lasted months.

Getting Paid for Jury Service. Each juror receives six dollars a day for every day that they appear. If you are selected to serve on a case you will get ten dollars a day for every day that you are seated in that trial. Now don't get all excited, hopefully that will pay for your lunch, maybe.

The long and the short of it is that it is one more right you have, so use it, don't let the government use or abuse it, if you do nothing else to get involved, do this one task that makes the whole system work. Just do it.

The Student Body of Law

SELECTIVE SERVICE - THE DRAFT

Most people see this as a patriotic right of passage; some see it as contemptible

That's right, once you men turn eighteen, you're obligated to register for the draft. You can do this at any U.S. Post Office and it only takes a couple of minutes. Some schools require it for admission. Most people see this as a patriotic right of passage; some see it as contemptible; some may not even know "There was one?" referring to the statement of "Cruiser" in the movie STRIPES. Just in case you were wondering, there is no draft and there hasn't been one since the '70's. Even back then, so long as you were in school, you couldn't be drafted, so don't worry, if this changes, you will probably hear about it well in advance. You have probably heard about it from your dad, grandfather, or uncles, studied it in school, or heard such references in the movies, but never really gave it much thought. This section is mainly for the guys, since women have never been subject to forced military service and are exempt from registration. Although women are exempt from the draft, the U.S. military is certainly open to the female citizenry and will gladly accept your enlistment, should you desire to do so.

For those of you who don't know about Selective Service (the draft) and the registration requirement, here we go. The registration requirement and the draft has been the backup system to muster emergency military manpower to the U.S. military for more than fifty years. President Franklin Roosevelt signed the Selective Training and Service Act of 1940, which created the first peacetime draft in this country and was done in anticipation of the demands for manpower that World War II would make. It also established the Selective Service System as an independent federal agency within the executive branch of the federal government.

Even after the war, men were drafted to run the military and various military campaigns from 1948 through 1973 (i.e. Korea & Viet Nam). Elvis was even drafted in the '50's and Muhammad Ali in the '60's. As the Viet Nam war was winding down, the then controversial draft ended in 1973 and the era of the All-Volunteer military began, ending the registration requirement.

Escalating tensions in the middle-east in 1980, specifically the Soviet invasion of Afghanistan and the Iran hostage-taking, caused President Jimmy Carter to re-institute the registration requirements, which remains as insurance just in case our country needs military personnel in a hurry.

The Military Selective Service Act governs the operations of the Selective Service System and requires men to register when they turn eighteen. In order to register, you simply provide the Selective Service System with personal information, such as name, address, date of birth, and Social Security Account Number. Even though no one is currently being drafted, it is a civic and legal responsibility. Don't worry, registering with Selective Service does not mean that you are joining the military, but it does mean that the U.S. government wants to know who you are and where you are when you turn eighteen, just in case the government decides they need forced military personnel.

Failure to register and comply with the Military Selective Service Act is actually punishable by a fine of up to $250,000, imprisonment for up to five years, or both. That's not to say that this particular crime is widely prosecuted, but the law is there nonetheless, and federal and certain state laws may require registration as a prerequisite for obtaining student financial aid, job training, government employment, or U.S. naturalization.

DO YOU HAVE TO REGISTER?

Probably so, with few exceptions, all male United States citizens and male aliens residing in the United States and its territories must register within thirty days of their eighteenth birthday. Parolees, refugees, and applicants for asylum are considered to be residents of the United States and therefore must register within thirty days of their eighteenth birthday. Even disabled men who are able to function in public, with or without assistance, must register. A friend or relative may help a disabled man complete the registration form if he is unable to do so himself. The law does exempt certain persons from registering: 1) Females; 2) Lawfully admitted non-immigrant aliens (such as those men on visitor or student visas and members of diplomatic or trade missions and their families) because they are residing in this country temporarily; 3) Men who are unable to register due to circumstances beyond their control, such as being hospitalized, institutionalized, or incarcerated. However, they must register within thirty days after their release; 4) Members of the Armed Forces on full-time active duty. This exemption also applies to cadets and midshipmen at the United States service academies. However, upon release from active duty, a man must register within thirty

The Student Body of Law

days if he is not yet twenty-six years of age and has not already registered.

The law even requires that you keep the information in your registration record up to date, even notifying Selective Service each time you move within ten days of the relocation. Again, this requirement is not readily enforced, but again it is a requirement. This only applies to men ages eighteen through twenty-five, after you reach age twenty-six, there is no requirement to update your registration record.

WHY DO I NEED TO COMPLY?

As stated earlier, it is the law, albeit one that is not actively prosecuted, nonetheless Federal and many state laws require registration-age men to be registered with Selective Service to remain eligible for applying for the following benefits: 1) student financial aid; 2) government employment; 3) employment with the U.S. Postal Service; 4) job training; and, 5) U.S. citizenship for male immigrants.

HOW TO REGISTER?

There are several ways a young man can register with the Selective Service System:

1. On-Line: register by clicking on the "Register On-Line Now" icon at the Selective Service web site (www.sss.gov);
2. The U.S. Post Office: pick up a Registration Form, SSS Form 1M(UPO), complete and sign it, and mail it (don't forget the stamp);
3. U.S. Embassy or Consulate: a U.S. citizen living or visiting overseas at the time you are required to register, go to the nearest U.S. Embassy or Consular office where personnel will assist you in registering.

You are not officially registered until your registration information is entered into the Selective Service registration file and you have been assigned a Selective Service Number.

You will then receive in the mail a Registration Acknowledgment Card showing the information recorded in your registration file, your Selective Service Number, and a Change of Information Form. If any of the information on your Registration Acknowledgment Card is incorrect, it is important that you correct it and mail the Change of Information Form back to Selective Service. You should keep the registration acknowledgment in a safe place as proof of your registration.

If you do not receive your Registration Acknowledgment Card within ninety days of the date you completed your registration form, it is important that you write to the following address or call (847) 688-6888:

> Selective Service System
> Registration Information Office
> Post Office Box 94638
> Palatine, IL 60064-4638

Verification of your registration and/or change of information can be done on-line at www.sss.gov.

WHO WOULD BE DRAFTED IF THE DRAFT WERE RE-INSTITUTED?

Excellent question. According to the guidelines currently in place, men who will reach age twenty during the calendar year in which inductions occur would be the first group to be called. If more men are needed that year, after all men turning twenty are considered, the order of call would continue up to those who will reach age twenty-one, then twenty-two, and on up through age twenty-five. The order of inductions within each age group would he determined by a lottery which matches a random sequence number with birth dates.

If you were ever selected for induction, you would be sent an Order to Report for Induction along with detailed instructions explaining where to report and what actions would be required on your part to fulfill this requirement. There are instances and circumstances that relieve you from going into the service if you file a claim for postponement or reclassification. If so, your induction would be delayed until a decision is made on whether the claim is accepted or denied. Some examples of the requirements to obtain a postponement or a reclassification are as follows:

Postponements: 1) full-time college students who desire to finish their current semester; 2) full-time college students in their last academic year who desire to finish that academic year; 3) high school students not yet twenty years old who desire to stay in school until they graduate.

Reclassifications: 1) men whose induction would create a hardship to their dependents 2) students studying for the ministry; 3) ministers of religion; 4) Conscientious Objectors (those who hold deep religious, moral, or

The Student Body of Law

ethical beliefs against participation in war).

If the objection is to participate in combat military service only, one would be inducted to perform only non-combat military service; if the objection is to participate in all military service, in lieu of induction one would be ordered to perform civilian work contributing to the maintenance of the national health, safety, or interest as determined by the Director of Selective Service).

The moral of the story is, if you're in school, stay there until they give you your degree. You never know when a war may break out. God forbid it's right after the semester you decided that catching rays, drinking beer, and staying out all night was a better choice than going to class every now and then. Hello, Uncle Sam. By the way, those with college degrees are historically inducted as officers, whereas the others go in at the lowest rank. Education has all kinds of pay-offs.

CIGARETTES & TOBACCO

Congratulations, you have turned eighteen and can now legally possess tobacco products. As you are probably aware if you're reading this section, it is illegal in Texas and many, if not all states, to possess tobacco products if you are under the age of eighteen. This can even impact your privilege to drive by causing license suspension in some instances. One other thing; now that you are away from home and away from many constraints, this is a time you may form habits that may very well stick with you for many, many years. I don't have to tell you about tobacco's effects on health and I certainly won't preach to you, but it is worth being said one more time, it is a habit that can become very difficult to kick and could ultimately kill you in a very unpleasant way.

DRIVER'S LICENSE

You must have a valid driver's license to drive, even for a motorcycle or scooter. It also acts as proper identification.

New to Texas & over eighteen - A new resident moving into Texas who has a valid driver's license from his home state, has thirty days after entry into the state to secure a Texas driver's license. In addition to testing, all first time original applicants must visit a Texas Driver's License office. If you have been previously licensed in another state, you'll need:

    1) Proof of Identity, Social Security Number, & Texas vehicle registration and liability insurance, if you own a vehicle;

2) Complete all required forms available at any Texas Driver License office;
3) Pay the required fee;
4) Pass the vision exam;
5) Appear for photograph and thumbprints; however, thumbprints are not included on the driver license;
6) If you have a VALID out-of-state license in your possession, please bring it to the driver license office to surrender;
7) If you have an EXPIRED out-of-state license, you will be required to pass both the written and driving exams, in addition to a vision test. (You must provide the vehicle for the road test).

Never had a license? If you are a new resident from out-of-country or never been licensed, it's the same as above, but if you do not have a Social Security Number, you will need to complete a Social Security Affidavit. Renewal? You may renew your Texas Driver License up to one year prior to the current expiration date and can renew online, by telephone, or by mail or in person at any Texas Driver's License office. You will be required to present proof of identity and proof of Social Security number, pass the vision exam, and pay the required fees. If your Texas driver's license has been expired for more than two years, you must appear in person at any Texas Driver License office and apply as an original applicant.

"AUTOMATIC" DRIVER'S LICENSE SUSPENSIONS – UNDER 21

Minors get hit much harder for the same sort of suspensions that do those over twenty-one. "Automatic" suspensions occur when a minor is convicted for the offenses detailed in the section Driver's License Suspensions in Chapter 9, just like those over twenty-one, but usually have a longer suspension period. There are also additional situations that apply only to those under twenty-one, such as: DWI (alcohol); Intoxication Assault; Intoxication Manslaughter; Purchase, Attempt to Purchase, Consumption or Possession of Alcohol by Minor; Misrepresentation of Age by a Minor; Driving Under the Influence of Alcohol (DUI), which means with any "detectable" amount of alcohol); and, Any Drug Offense, which includes Possession, Manufacture or Delivery of any Drug/Controlled Substance/Dangerous Drug/Volatile Chemical. There are usually other things you will have to do, like attend an educational class before DPS will reinstate your driver's license.

CHAPTER SIX
"Let's Party!"

This is probably the chapter you have all turned to right off the bat, maybe even while standing in the bookstore. No matter, this is maybe the first time you have been truly on your own — that is to say no curfew, no house rules, no household chores, and especially no parents keeping tabs on your whereabouts. This is definitely a time in your life where you are wanting to let your hair down, sew your oats, stretch your boundaries, go wild, or whatever you want to call it. I'm not here to tell you what to do or not do, but there are some things you need to know about the law that may affect when, where, and what you are or thinking about doing.

"LET'S HAVE A PARTY"

That's how it usually starts and always sounds like an excellent idea, but sometimes can cause some headaches for the host or hostess. Obviously, when you open your home, either to select friends or the campus in general for an open party, your home is at risk. If you don't know, sometimes at parties people can act a little more, let's say, *free* with your house and furnishings than they might at their own home. Granted, you don't want to be the party wrecker, but a little preparation may prevent some problems later. If you are going to have people in and out and throughout your house or apartment, you may want to hide anything that you don't want walking off or accidentally getting broken, such as jewelry and other small valuables and breakables. Don't get me wrong, I'm not paranoid, but sometimes people may show-up that you don't know and you can't and don't want to watch out for everyone and everything, so protect what you can and enjoy the party.

NOISE & MUSIC

One man's music is another man's noise. No matter the artistic attributes and entertainment value of the music, most cities and towns have some form of noise ordinance. These rules are extremely subjective and are usually in place as a tool for the local authorities to use to discourage loud music and wild parties. To their credit, most local police agencies have a policy of warning the owners at least once before they write a ticket for the Class C offense. After that, if the noise continues, they may take the position that it is breach of the peace and start arresting people to control the situation. The best bet is to try to keep it low enough that they don't ever come. If they do, turn it down and hopefully they will go away.

THE NEIGHBORS

Another little thing that may keep the cops from coming early or at all is to invite the neighbors, or at least give them a day or two notice that you may be having a soirée. Either they will join in the revelry or they will find other plans that take them out away from the loud music, crowd, and traffic.

THE POLICE ARE AT THE FRONT DOOR

This is one area that is going to be up to you, to be calm, polite, and deal with them as best you can. Refer to the earlier chapters regarding Search & Seizure and Some Good Advice Concerning the Police, as well as your Legal Rights and you should do just fine, but rely on your own good judgment. Sometimes, you are going to have to break up the party yourself and move on. If this happens, always be careful that the police are not just waiting around the corner or down the road to stop you or your guests. Don't give them any reason or opportunity to do so.

PROVIDING THE ALCOHOL
CIVIL LIABILITY

It's called the Texas Dram Shop Act and is in Section 2.02 of the Texas Alcohol & Beverage Code. This law makes it illegal to provide, sell, or serve an alcoholic drink/beverage to an obviously intoxicated customer, making the "provider" of alcohol potentially liable for any harm or injury caused by the "obviously intoxicated" customer. One can recover monetary damages for violating the Dram Shop Law from a bar, club, restaurant, or convenience store who serves or sells an "obviously intoxicated" person if: 1) it was apparent to the provider that the individual being sold, served, or provided with an alcoholic beverage was obviously intoxicated to the extent that he presented a clear danger to himself and others; and 2) the intoxication of the recipient of the alcoholic beverage was a proximate cause of the damages suffered.

The Student Body of Law

The Dram Shop law only applies to liquor license holders, such as nightclubs, bars, convenience stores, and grocery stores, not private individuals or "social hosts". The Dram Shop Law is most commonly used to sue a bar, club, or store who served or sold alcohol to someone who then injures or kills someone later, such as someone that is hit by an intoxicated driver. This sounds like it would be an easy lawsuit to prove, but the injured party must show that the person who served the drunk knew the person was "obviously intoxicated" and "presented a clear danger to himself or others" when served.

Taking this law to the extreme can lead to some unique possibilities. For instance, Joe and his buddy, Buddy, go out for a night of drinking. After a couple or ten beers at the local watering hole, the two have a disagreement and end up in a fight in the parking lot. Joe gets the best of Buddy and knocks three of his teeth out. BANG, Joe's buddy may have some cause to sue the bar for his teeth, if he can demonstrate that the bar served Joe when he was "obviously intoxicated". Now this does not even consider any contributory negligence of Buddy, but is merely an extreme example. This may also spill over into situations involving minors. Let's say Buddy is underage and then gets into his truck and ultimately hits a telephone pole and knocks the rest of his teeth out. BANG, he may even be able to successfully sue the bar for the injuries he causes himself. Some states, not Texas, even extend this liability to serving "habitually intoxicated" people. Let's say Buddy's uncle, Cooter Brown, who everyone knows is always drunk, comes in for a drink every day and has a few. Over time, Uncle Cooter has squandered the family fortune and due to his drunkenness, the family business also goes under. The family may even be able to argue that the bar serving him "caused" Uncle Cooter to piss away his family's fortunes. These are extreme cases but within the realm of possibilities.

The Texas Dram Shop law does not apply to party guests or social occasions where they are not sold the drinks. That's not to say absolutely no liability may come from the kegger Joe has almost every Friday night, such as allowing underage people to drink, but not under the Dram Shop Law for their actions later. Although a party giver may not have this legal liability, the best practice is for a good host to always keep control over his guests and make sure that if they do become intoxicated they try to make sure their intoxicated guests avoid doing something foolish, like driving. Take control and have a friend or cab take them home, just for safe measure.

CRIMINAL LIABILITY

This is where things get tricky. Providing alcohol to a minor is a Class A Misdemeanor, even if you are a minor. This is really the major concern when throwing a party. Unless you monitor everyone there, dole out the refreshments to only those who are twenty-one or older and rule the party with an iron fist, someone under twenty-one may be having a drink on you. Whether or not the charge can be proven in a court of law, local police officers regularly charge the party throwers to discourage their fun. Even though it is a shaky or weak case, it can result in your spending the night and making bail. As for those twenty-one and over, generally speaking, they are responsible for their own drinking and behavior, not you.

FURNISHING ALCOHOL TO A MINOR

Scenario Number One: Your girlfriend's little brother makes you a deal: his friends will give you the money, plus fifty bucks, if you go buy the beer for their party. When they are busted in their dorm room for being totally out of control, one of them lets it slip that you bought the beer. BANG.

Scenario Number Two: You are in the middle of your apartment packed to the gills with hot chicks, dancing the night away. Everyone is helping themselves to the keg on the back porch, when the cops show up, start writing tickets, and arresting people for MIP and public intoxication. BANG, BANG.

Scenario Number 3: You are out on the town and meet this hot girl who is in the club without the "over 21 wristband". No worries. You buy the drinks and give them to her and her friends. When TABC wanders through the club, they see her and her friends drinking and ask who bought the drinks. One of her friends points you out. BANG, BANG, BANG.

In each scenario, you may be arrested for "contributing to a minor". Under the Texas Alcohol & Beverage Code, you may be charged with this offense if you purchase, give or even make available an alcoholic beverage to a minor (someone under twenty-one). The exception to this is that you can make a purchase, or give or make alcohol available to someone who is your

The Student Body of Law

child if you are visibly present when the minor possess or consumes the alcohol, otherwise it is a Class B Misdemeanor.

BEER, WINE & COCKTAILS
A HISTORY OF DRINK

Intoxicating drink has been produced and consumed by humans for centuries. In the time of Beowulf, the Vikings drank what was called "mead", which was a strong beer/wine like liquid. The Greeks and Romans drank vast quantities of wine. Monks first perfected the beverage we now know as beer. Strong drink has always been relied upon by man to toast special occasions, console the spirits, woo women, celebrate, and relax with friends, but its overindulgence has also been extremely destructive to many people's lives and been the cause of death and unhappiness of an extremely large segment of our population.

Alcohol is the most widely accepted and abused drug in our society. The Federal Government tried to legislate morality and extinguish alcohol from existence in 1920 with the 18th Amendment to the U.S. Constitution and its companion "The Volstad Act" making it illegal to manufacture, possess, or consume intoxicating beverages. This social experiment was a huge failure, giving rise to bootlegging and the speakeasy bars of the Roaring 20's. It was also one of the first areas of business organized by the so-called mob, establishing the first substantial accumulation of wealth for organized crime. Congress ultimately repealed the 21st Amendment in 1933 during the depths of The Great Depression.

ALCOHOL'S HISTORICAL TIMELINE

DATE(S)	EVENT(S)
6000-4000 BC	The selective cultivation of grape vines for making wine ("Viticulture"), is believed to have originated in the mountains between the Black and Caspian seas (modern day Armenia).
c. 3000 BC	According to recipes found on clay tablets, Sumeria/Mesopotamian civilization (modern day Iraq) enjoy over twenty varieties of beer.
3000-1000 BC	Wine production is refined and the wine trade becomes an important part of commerce and culture in the Mediterranean.

1800 BC	Beer is produced in quantity in northern Syria.
1500 BC	Commercial wine production emerges in the Levant and Aegean.
900-800 BC	Large-scale production of wine emerges as extensive vineyards in Assyria (modern day Iraq) to accommodate the growing wine drinking population.
c. 800 BC	Distillation of barley and rice beer is practiced in India.
c. 50 BC	Dionysius of Halicarnassus writes "the Gauls (French) have no knowledge of wine… but used a foul-smelling liquour made of barley rotted in water (beer)."
c. 500 AD	Wine reaches Tang China through the Silk Road trade routes.
768 AD	First specific reference to the use of hops in beer, Abbey St. Denis in France by King Pepin le Bref.
1100 AD	Alcohol distillation is documented by the medical school at Salerno, Italy. The product of the distillation is named 'spirits' in reference to it being the extracted spirit of the wine. Middle Ages Alcohol distillation emerges in Europe.
C1500	"Alcohol" is the term used for distilled spirits, rather than its previous general meaning of any product of vaporization and condensation emerges.
1516 AD	German Beer Purity Law ("Rheinheitsgebot") makes it illegal to make beer with anything but barley, hops, and pure water.
1525-1550	Excessive drinking of distilled spirits become apparent in England.
1524-1556	Vitriculture spreads through South America.
1550-1575	Drunkenness emerges as a criminal act in Elizabethan England, as well as in the Colonies of America.
1600's	Use of alcohol, as well as hashish and opium becomes widespread in Constantinople.
1600-1625	Drunkenness from beer and wine becomes more widespread and is prevalent throughout the classes.
1606	Parliament passes "the Act to Repress the Odious and Loathsome Sin of Drunkenness"
1637	Each town in Massachusetts is ordered to establish a man to sell wines and "strong water" so that the public will not suf-

The Student Body of Law

	fer from lack of proper accommodations.
1643	Britain imposes an excise tax on distilled spirits and the "moonshine" trade is born.
1649	Inns in Massachusetts are required to provide beer for entertainment.
c. 1650	New England colonies attempt to establish a precise definition of drunkenness that includes the time spent drinking, amount, and behavior.
1650-1675	Gin (distilled grain with the juniper berry) is born in Holland and spreads rapidly to England by British soldiers.
1672	A law forbidding the payment of wages in the form of alcohol results in a labor strike.
1600's	France emerges as a leader in quality cognac production.
1700's	Scotland and Ireland establishes reputation as quality whiskey makers.
1770's	Vitriculture established in California.
1791	"The Act of 1791" (better known as the "Whiskey Tax") enacted on both publicly and privately distilled whiskey.
1793	The "Whiskey Rebellion" of Pennslyvania occurs, government troops are used to arrest a handful of distillery leaders refusing to pay taxes on their products.
1802	The "Whiskey Tax" is repealed by Thomas Jefferson who called it 'infernal,' and 'hostile to the genius of a free people'
1814-1817	A temporary tax on alcohol is enacted to help pay for the War of 1812.
1862	"The Act of July 1" is enacted by Abraham Lincoln, imposing a tax on liquor to help pay for the Civil War. This act also created the Office of Internal Revenue. The alcohol tax began at 20 cents per gallon in 1862 and rose to $2.00 per gallon just over two years later.
1907	The Pure Food and Drug Act passes, regulating the labeling of products containing Alcohol, Opiates, Cocaine, and Cannabis, among others.
1920	The 18th Amendment (prohibition amendment) takes effect, prohibiting the manufacture, sale, transportation, import, and export of intoxicating liquors for beverage pur-

	poses, as does "the Volsted Act" that makes possession and consumption illegal as well.
1920-1933	"Prohibition" in the US. Alcohol sales continue, the bootlegging, smuggling, moonshine and other underground industries boom.
1933	Prohibition ends with the passage of the 21st Amendment.
1933-1970	With the return of the excise tax on alcohol at $2.00 per gallon in 1934; $3.00 in 1940; $4.00 in 1941; $6.00 in 1942; $9.00 in 1944, and $10.50 in 1970.
1978	US President Jimmy Carter signs bill legalizing home brewing of beer for the first time since Prohibition.

Resources / References
1. Courtwright, DT. Forces of Habit. Harvard U. Press, 2001,
2. Walton S, Glover B. The Ultimate Encyclopedia of Wine, Beer, Spirits, & Liqueurs. Hermes, 1999.
3. Sherratt A. "Alcohol and Its Alternatives - Symbol and substance in pre-industrial cultures." Consuming Habits. Routledge, 1995.
4. Escohotado A. A Brief History of Drugs. Park Street, 1999.
5. "2000 BC Cuneiform Tablets Have Beer Recipe." AP Story, Nov 12, 2001.
6. http://hbd.org/brewery/library/ReinHeit.html and
   http://members.aol.com/carlaac1/private/victor/viti4.html
7. Austin, G. A Chronology of Psychoactive Substance Use.
8. Nelson D. Moonshiners, Bootleggers, & Rumrunners. Motorbooks, 1995.
9. Pure Food and Drug Act (1906)
10. McCarthy, RG. Drinking and Intoxication. New College and Univ Press. 1963.
11. Bonnie RJ, Whitebread CH II. The Marijuana Conviction: A History of Marijuana Prohibition in the United States. Lindesmith, 1999.
12. U.S. Constitution
13. By permission of http://www.erowid.org/chemicals/alcohol/alcohol_timeline.php3

ALCOHOL IN GENERAL

Not often thought of as a drug, alcohol is classified as a Sedative/Hypnotic. It is also one of the most abused addictive substances used by Americans, especially college students. Alcohol contributes to health problems resulting in death and complications more than any other drug. Notwithstanding its legalities, compulsive drinking in excess, commonly referred to as "binge drinking," has become a serious problem, especially on college campuses.

Ethyl alcohol, or ethanol, is the kind of alcohol you can drink and is produced by fermenting or distilling a clear, colorless liquid from various fruits, vegetables, or grains. Alcoholic beverages get their color from the diluents, additives, and by-products of fermentation and aging. The alcohol content varies, depending on the type of alcoholic beverage you're drinking. Beer is generally contains about 5% alcohol by volume (or 3.5% in light beer); Wine

The Student Body of Law

is generally between 10% and 14% alcohol content; Fortified Wines such as sherry, port, and vermouth contain between 14% and 20%; and Distilled Spirits (whisky, vodka, rum, gin) are first fermented, then distilled to raise the alcohol content.

The effects of drinking do not depend on the type of alcoholic beverage, - but rather on the amount of alcohol consumed over a period of time. Alcohol is rapidly absorbed into the bloodstream from the small intestine and less from the stomach and colon. The drinker's blood alcohol concentration depends on:

1) the amount consumed in a given time;
2) size, sex, body build, and metabolism of the person; and
3) the type and amount of food in the stomach.

Once the alcohol has passed into the blood, food or beverage cannot diminish or interfere with its effects, however, fruit sugar can shorten the duration of alcohol's effect by speeding up metabolism and thus its ultimate elimination from the blood. The metabolic rate of the average adult is about 8.5 g of alcohol per hour (i.e. about two-thirds of a regular beer or about one shot per hour), but varies depending on the person's usual amount of drinking, physique, sex, liver size, and genetic factors.

"Binge drinking" has gained the attention of the media, school administrators, and the legal community in recent years. This type of drinking is apparently popular with the younger and more inexperienced drinkers in our society, particularly on the college campus scene. Whether or not this is a new attitude of drinking or just a name given to something that has been done for decades on U.S. college campuses is irrelevant. It is the danger of extremely large amounts of consumption that is important and can be a serious threat. It is possible for a person to consume so much alcohol in a short amount of time that he/she poisons him/herself to the point that the body goes into shock and various body functions begin to shut down. Death is very real possibility in these circumstances. It is extremely important for anyone who sees an individual who is consuming alcohol in an unusually large or quick fashion to step in and remedy the situation or assist that person with medical attention or supervision.

Drinking heavily over a short period of time usually results in a "hangover": headache, nausea, shakiness, and sometimes vomiting, beginning from eight to twelve hours later. A hangover is due partly to poisoning by alcohol, the components of the drink, and partly to the body's reaction to withdrawal from alcohol. Although there are dozens of home remedies suggested for hangovers, there is currently no known effective cure.

Combining alcohol with other drugs can make the effects of these other drugs much stronger and more dangerous. Many accidental deaths have occurred after people have used alcohol combined with other drugs. Alcohol should be avoided if taking any types of tranquillizers, barbiturates and other sleeping pills, or antihistamines (in cold, cough, and allergy remedies).

Years of alcohol use can reveal the long-term effects, but they may appear after only months of heavy drinking. Chronic alcohol consumption can bring on serious negative physical and psychological problems that are potentially life-threatening, such as heart and liver disease, inflammation of the stomach, loss of appetite, vitamin deficiencies, and infection. Even moderate drinking can generate psychological dependence. This is seen in people who only drink under certain conditions, such as before and during certain social occasions, which usually suggests a type of dependence more for the craving of the alcohol's psychological effects, such as relaxation or anxiety relief, not necessarily the intoxication itself.

Heavy drinkers begin to experience a physical dependence because their bodies have adapted to the alcohol and suffer withdrawal symptoms if they suddenly stop drinking. Withdrawal symptoms range from jumpiness, sleeplessness, sweating and poor appetite, to tremors, convulsions, hallucinations, and sometimes even death.

LEGAL DRINKING AGE

In the '70's, the legal drinking age was eighteen. In the early '80's, it was raised to nineteen for a brief period time and ultimately jumped to twenty-one a few years later. The Federal Government has held the states hostage by threatening to withhold federal highway funds from states that didn't raise the legal drinking age. In response to pressures by special interest groups such as M.A.D.D. (Mothers Against Drunk Driving) and others, state legislatures have increasingly tightened the DWI laws, including lowering the legal blood/breath alcohol concentration, which again has been lowered across the country in response to special interests and the Federal Government's threats. In Texas and most states, the legal drinking age is twenty-one years old. Oddly enough, a person can work in a bar or restaurant and serve alcohol at eighteen, but cannot consume what they serve. A minor can legally consume

The Student Body of Law

an alcoholic beverage in Texas, but only if the minor is in the visible presence of the minor's adult parent, guardian, or spouse.

TEXAS ALCOHOLIC BEVERAGE COMMISSION

Otherwise known as the TABC. Agents from TABC are peace officers, just like a sheriff or a city policeman, but they have no more authority to search and arrest than any other peace officers, and have no more authority under the law to enter and search a private residence and arrest an occupant on "minor in possession" (MIP) charges. If a police officer is invited into a private home or if the officer's presence in the home is authorized in some manner and the officer sees a crime committed, he may make an arrest for any offense committed in his presence, including MIP.

A warrant to search a home for a specific item of contraband or evidence of a crime requires only one affidavit stating the facts supporting the probable cause, but to search for an illicit can of beer or other Texas Alcoholic Beverage Code violations require affidavits from two credible persons.

Any peace officer (including TABC agents) may search a premise covered by a license or permit to serve alcohol without a search warrant. No peace officer in Texas, including a TABC Agent, is authorized to enter a home for the purpose of arrest and/or search for minors in possession of alcohol without a warrant, nor may they conduct a search of your home based upon suspicion that minors in your home are in illegal possession of alcohol. Entry is only lawful if by a warrant, by your permission, or if a crime is committed in the officer's presence. An officer may knock on the door and ask permission to conduct a search, but "suspicion" alone does not give them the authority to enter or search a private home.

WHEN CAN I BUY?

Assuming you're twenty-one years of age or older.

BEER, WINE & COCKTAILS

Starting at 7a.m. until midnight on any day except Sunday. On Sundays, you can buy beer from midnight to 1 a.m.; noon to midnight; and between 10:00a.m. and noon if the beer is served to a customer during the service of food. There are other late hour and on-premises license holder exceptions that allow clubs and other similar places to sell until 2:00a.m.

LIQUOR

Generally speaking, from 10a.m. until 9p.m., except on Sunday, Thanksgiving, Christmas, and New Year's Day. When these holidays fall on a Sunday, the sale of liquor is prohibited on the following Monday also.

WHERE CAN I DRINK?
AT HOME

Anytime you want, so long as it is not in a public place.

PUBLIC PLACES

Anytime except on Sunday between 1:15a.m. and 12 noon or on any other day between 12:15a.m. and 7a.m.

BARS & CLUBS

These places usually hold licenses that make them "extended hours areas", which extend the public place hours on these premises. This allows you to drink your drinks after closing time at the club for fifteen minutes, extending the allowable consumption period to 2:15a.m. Basically, if you can buy it, you've got at least fifteen minutes to suck it down. Otherwise it is a Class C Misdemeanor.

TAILGATING & SPORTS VENUES

I fondly refer to this as the "Texan Tailgating Law". As you can see above, if you are a fan of professional football, drinking before a noon game can be problematic if you are overly concerned with the law. Being a devoted Houston Texan fan and avid tailgater, this posed a problem for my crew during the Texans' first two seasons. However, in January 2004, an exception to the hours of consumption on Sunday was enacted which allowed a person to begin consuming alcoholic beverages at a sports venue at 10a.m., which includes the parking lot. This law does not totally remedy the problem, because the gates open at 8 a.m., but it's a start.

IDENTIFICATION
FAILURE TO IDENTIFY

While at a big party, the cops arrive and shut down the scene. They instruct everyone to leave, but on your way out and although you have done absolute-

The Student Body of Law

ly nothing, the officer stops you and asks you for ID. Not only because you are underage, but because you feel you are being singled out and hassled, you decide to refuse the officer's request. You know you don't have to carry a driver's license or other ID if you're not driving, so you refuse, just to spite the officer. If you've just been detained, not arrested, you don't have to give them squat, but refusing to identify might cause them to arrest you anyway and take you downtown so they can determine who you really are. If this happens, you still won't be charged with failing to carry ID, because there is no such crime.

If you've been arrested, you have to give your name, address, and date of birth to a police officer who requests it. The police will ask you for a lot more than this, but these three items are all you're legally required to give them. If you refuse to do so, you will probably be charged with the Class C Misdemeanor offense of Failure to Identify.

Instead of refusing altogether, you tell him you don't have any ID and that your name is Mickey Mouse, from Orlando, Florida. BANG, you're under arrest for giving a false or fictitious name, residence address, or date of birth if the peace officer has lawfully arrested or detained you or has good cause to believe you are a witness to a criminal offense. This is a Class B Misdemeanor.

Realizing that you have a warrant for your arrest from the speeding ticket you ignored last semester, you either refuse to give the ID information or give false info. The offense you may be charged with is raised one level because of the warrant. You are "a fugitive from justice" when you committed the offense.

If you've been arrested, you have to give your name, address, and date of birth to a police officer who requests it.

FAKE ID

You didn't go see Crazy Lola (See Chapter 14), but you have started a little collection of IDs from older brothers and friends for use on occasion to get into clubs and such. You are stopped one night and as you're getting your real ID out, several others accidentally fall on the ground. BANG, you are arrested for possessing multiple IDs.

It is illegal to possess more than one currently valid driver's license or provide a false name or address, or make a false statement or commit fraud when applying for an original, renewal or duplicate driver's license. It is also illegal to lend a driver's license to or permit someone else to use your license, nor can you display or represent as your own a driver's license not issued to you. These offenses are Misdemeanors.

This time when the cops bust the party, you are ready. You went to see Crazy Lola (refer to Chapter 14) and got one of her famous perfect fake IDs, complete with your own picture, name, address, and date of birth, with two years added to boot. It's perfect. You flip the ID to the cop and he runs the info. He discovers the discrepancy between your ID and the state's database and investigates further. BANG, BANG, you are under arrest for tampering with government record.

Anyone who makes, presents, or uses any record, document, government record, or thing with knowledge of its falsity and with intent that it be taken as a genuine governmental record commits a Class A Misdemeanor, unless the actor's intent is to defraud or harm another, in which event the offense is a State Jail felony.

DWI

Driving While Intoxicated (DWI) is the most frequently prosecuted misdemeanor offense in the State of Texas and probably nationwide. It is also the one with some of the most damaging and far-reaching ramifications to a citizen's everyday life, if convicted. An important area of concern to anyone who drinks is DWI and as a practical matter, the safest policy, legalities aside, is don't drink and drive. Take a cab or walk if you can. That being said, it is not illegal in Texas to drink and then drive. It is illegal to consume alcoholic beverages or even have an open container of an alcoholic beverage in the vehicle while driving, including the passengers. Only recently has this become law in Texas. What gets you in trouble is when you are driving after drinking so much, that you have become intoxicated. In Texas, it is illegal to operate a motor vehicle in a public place while either having a blood/breath alcohol concentration of .08 or higher or having lost the normal use of one's mental or physical faculties by the introduction of alcohol into one's body. That is a long, but important definition of DWI law in Texas.

That being said, it is extremely important to try and prevent the first DWI conviction, if at all possible by defending the charge. Many people make the potentially fatal mistake of failing to defend themselves in a first offense DWI — because first offenders are typically offered a relatively light punish-

The Student Body of Law

ment involving probation — under the assumption that they do not intend to ever place themselves in a position of being charged a second time. Unfortunately, they do not truly realize that due to the extremely subjective nature of the charge (i.e. the Peace Officer's opinion that someone is intoxicated) when a citizen is stopped on a minor traffic violation and might have had a beer or glass of wine with dinner, if the officer smells an odor of an alcoholic beverage and then runs the driver's license, discovering the prior DWI, that citizen's chance of being arrested and charged with DWI again is extremely high.

LEGALLY INTOXICATED

What is intoxicated? In Texas, it is having a blood/breath alcohol concentration of .08 or higher, or loss of the normal use of one's mental or physical faculties by the introduction of alcohol into one's body.

Remember also, that anything you do can be later used to prosecute you and may even be on videotape

A public place is just about anywhere you can drive a car or truck except maybe on one's own or someone else's property that is not open to the public (i.e. ranch land, hunting leases, private driveways or roads, etc). This includes just about everywhere else, including parking lots and driveways. A motor vehicle is everything you think it probably would be: cars, trucks, motorcycles, dune buggies, tractors, trolleys, scooters, mopeds, vespas — if it has a motor, it is probably considered a motor vehicle, even a golf cart. This even includes boats.

Operating means driving, but it also includes situations where people have been found in the driver's seat after an accident and even passed out at traffic lights with the foot on the brake. This is not an area of distinction you truly want to fool with, again the best policy is don't drink and drive.

So, you have been at a bar or party, it's late at night, and you are now driving home. Whether you are snot-slinging drunk, a little buzzed, or just had two or three beers, you need to know how to conduct yourself and what rights you have if stopped by a police officer. If you are stopped, you must present a valid Texas driver's license, and proof of valid insurance. You must comply with the officer's requests to get out of the car, stand where you are directed, and follow the officers commands concerning arrest. Other than that, you really don't have to do much else. You do not have to answer any questions, you do not have to take any field sobriety tests, and you do not have to take a breathalyzer test. Remember, the officer on the street is always concerned for his/her own safety, so don't give them any reason to be apprehensive or nervous. No furtive movements or aggressive gestures or language. Remember also, that anything you do can be later used to prosecute you and may even be on videotape. Questions by the officer and the standardized field sobriety tasks are designed to gather evidence against you in an attempt to ultimately prosecute and convict you. Unfortunately, an officer's perceptions can be skewed or affected by his/her own personal views or interests. If you decide to answer questions and take tests, do not be surprised later that those things are used as evidence to prosecute you. Additionally, don't be surprised if what the officer testifies as to what you said or how you performed on the field sobriety test are not what you remember.

STUPID HUMAN TRICKS – ROADSIDE TESTS

"Field sobriety tests" are the tests the officers give to drivers they suspect are intoxicated. The great likelihood is that if an officer is asking you to take a test, he has already decided you are intoxicated and is just trying to confirm and further support this opinion. These tests are designed to detect minor motor skill mistakes and lack of attentiveness all interpreted as "loss of normal use of mental and/or physical faculties". The interpretations of the performance of these exercises are extremely subjective in nature. The truth is that there really isn't even a "passing" grade. You must make your own decision whether or not to take these tests based upon what you think is in your best interest, realizing that the entire battery of tests to be performed are really an exercise in evidence collection to ultimately convict you of DWI. These tests do not give credit for the citizen's adequate performance, only the incorrect portions or mistakes are evaluated and considered.

The tests that are most commonly administered are: 1) the Horizontal Gaze Nystagumus Test (HGN), which is when an officer asks the person to follow a pen or finger from side to side. They are looking for a twitching of the eye that indicates a presence of alcohol that arguably exacerbates this naturally occurring and ever-present condition; 2) The Walk and Turn is a "divided attention test" where they ask a person to take nine steps on a line, heel to

The Student Body of Law

toe, with arms at their side. They also ask the person to stand in an awkward position while giving them instructions that are very difficult to do; 3) In One Leg Stand, the subject must stand on one leg, with the other extended approximately six inches from the ground, arms at their side, and count to thirty. Try it. It's hard; 4) With the Rhomberg test, the subject stands with their head back and estimates (in their head) thirty seconds. Studies have shown that humans cannot internally keep time, much less accurately estimate thirty seconds. They are also watching to see if you sway during this test. Again, tilting of the head disrupts the inner ear function, which controls balance; 5) The Nose Touch is asking the person to tilt their head back, close their eyes, and touch their nose. There is no academic or scientific support for this test at all. Many of the tests and instructions are similar to the childhood game of Simon Says, which is designed to trick the person into doing something they didn't really mean to do. The testimony at trial will be that these mistakes are all signs of intoxication and demonstrate that you lost the normal use of either your mental or physical faculties.

The officer's observations and testing interpretation represents the vast majority of evidence presented in DWI trials. It is rare that an officer administers the field sobriety test and then lets someone get back in the car and drive home. If it has happened to you, you are lucky. One thing that seems to always be reported is that the officers become agitated or increasingly threatening when a citizen advises them that they are not going to submit to any testing. Just remember, it is your right to refuse. We will talk about license suspensions and whether or not to take a breath test a little later, but remember any and all statements you make will probably be used against you. There is no "passing" grade, merely observations that indicate loss of mental or physical faculties, so don't think you will ever pass the field sobriety tests.

Just remember, it is your right to refuse.

Lastly, the officer will be asking you some questions. What questions might be asked of you?

Where are you going?
Where have you been?
What time is it?
Have you been drinking?
How much?

May I search your vehicle?

All of these seem quite harmless, but each have the potential to be very damaging if presented in court the right way. Refer to Chapter 3 regarding your legal rights, especially the right to remain silent. You do not have to answer any questions, other than identification and insurance, nor do you need to complete any tests.

CLASSIC SIGNS OF INTOXICATION
What are the classic signs of intoxication that are found in almost every police officer's report?
- Weaving inside the lines
- Driving to fast, driving too slow
- Driving without lights on
- Braking too late
- Making a wide turn
- Running a stop sign or light
- Blood-shot and glassy eyes.
- Slurred or slow speech;
- "Mush mouthed"
- Unsteady on the feet
- Unsure balance
- Smell of alcohol on breath or person
- Leaning on car for balance

THE CRIME OF DWI
Every other offense in the State of Texas, murder, rape, incest with a barnyard animal just to name a few, if the sentence is probated cannot be used to enhance punishment of subsequent charges, with one notable exception, DWI, and cannot be disposed of through Deferred Adjudication either. A first conviction is a Class B Misdemeanor; a second charge is a Class A Misdemeanor and a third charge is a Felony of the 3rd Degree, with the very real potential of incarceration in the Texas Department of Criminal Justice: Institutional Division, better known as prison.

DWI is also one of the very few crimes that is based solely upon another person's opinion, rather than definitive evidence. Whether someone has lost the normal use of their mental or physical faculties is one of opinion, there-

The Student Body of Law

fore several different people may have completely different opinions regarding the person's guilt.

If you cause an accident while intoxicated and someone suffers serious bodily injury or God forbid, dies, then the offense you can be charged with is elevated to Intoxication Assault and/or Intoxication Manslaughter, Felonies of the 2nd and 1st degree, respectively. If there is a child in the car while the driver is intoxicated, it, too, is a felony offense.

Conviction of DWI carries with it a lot of extra baggage, such as mandatory license suspensions in certain situations, mandatory attendance of alcohol education classes, installation of an interlock device, not to mention insurance headaches, and $1,000.00 minimum "surcharge" assessment for license renewal for three years after conviction.

SHOULD I BLOW?

I can only tell you that unless I have had absolutely no alcohol in more than twenty-four hours, I would not take the test. Based upon my experiences in trial, consultations with experts in various medical, scientific, and legal fields of study, I do not feel that the Intoxilyzer 5000 and other similar machines are reliable enough to accurately detect blood alcohol levels based upon a breath sample sufficient to convince me to take one. See BLOW & GO / THE INTERLOCK DEVICE section for more info.

A blood test is a much more accurate test, but it also has some margin for error. If you decide to submit to a test, you may ask for a blood test, if that's your decision, but they must only comply if you can arrange for a person certified to do so — a doctor — within a very short period of time and often in the middle of the night. It usually is not a viable option.

WHAT HAPPENS IF I BLOW?

If you submit to a breath test and it shows a level of 0.08 or greater, you will be charged with DWI and you have given the prosecuting attorney a piece of evidence that they will attempt to demonstrate to the jury is extremely reliable and proves their case beyond a reasonable doubt. Your license will also probably be suspended for ninety days for a first time failure and the suspension periods increase with subsequent alcohol contacts. The suspension is not automatic, as explained in the HOW WILL THIS AFFECT MY DRIVER'S LICENSE section.

If you pass the test, it is important to understand that this will not guarantee you are let go and not charged with DWI. If you are under the limit, but show some alcohol, the state may simply argue that it only shows that you were under the limit when you took the test, but that due to absorption and elimination, your blood alcohol level was higher when you were driving earlier. If you pass without any alcohol detected, law enforcement will then call in a Drug Recognition Expert that will evaluate you and determine that you are under the influence of an unknown drug, most likely a central nervous system depressant, that has caused the loss of normal use of mental or physical faculties and the lack of presence of alcohol merely supports their subjective opinion they formed based on your performance of the field sobriety tests given earlier.

WHAT HAPPENS IF I DON'T?

If you refuse the test, your license may be suspended for 180 days and your refusal may be used against you. This suspension is not automatic as believed and stated by law enforcement officers, however, it is possible, after you request a hearing, the DPS may adequately prove the necessary elements to support the suspension, but is definitely not automatic. The most important advantage your refusal provides is that the state will have to rely on the "loss of normal use" definition of intoxication alone and will have no scientific evidence (i.e. breath test) supporting the police officer's subjective opinion.

CAN THEY MAKE ME DO IT?

NO, you can only be forced to submit blood for testing when there has been an accident where the driver has been arrested for DWI, and the driver's automobile was involved in an accident caused by the driver being intoxicated, and the officer reasonably believes a person has died or will die as a result of the accident. Otherwise, your consent or a warrent is required for any and all testing, whether blood, breath, or urine. Many times, where a driver suspected of DWI is taken to the hospital for minor treatment, the driver's medical records are regularly subpoenaed by the District Attorney's office to see if the hospital did any blood tests in the normal course of treatment that indicates alcohol or drug levels. If so, they then attempt to use those results as evidence in trial.

HOW WILL THIS AFFECT MY DRIVER'S LICENSE

That depends on your particular case and the ultimate disposition of that case.

The Student Body of Law

License suspensions from either a refusal to take or for failing a breath test are totally separate from the DWI prosecution and are an Administrative License Revocation (ALR) pursued through the administrative law function of the State Office of Administrative Hearings. The only instance where the outcome of a criminal prosecution affects an ALR license suspension is when a jury acquits the person charged or the case is dismissed on a breath test failure case. In that instance, the license suspension can be rescinded, but other dispositions of a DWI prosecution generally do not affect an ALR suspension. If convicted of DWI for the first time, only if there is no probation is the license suspended for one year, however if it is a probated sentence then there is no license suspension. All subsequent convictions, whether probated or not, will result in license suspension and the length of the suspension will depend on prior record and suspensions.

Your license will probably be confiscated if you either blow and fail or refuse, if not and your license is suspended, cancelled, disqualified, or revoked for any reason, DPS may require the license holder to surrender the license to DPS. If demand for surrender of the license is made by DPS and the license holder fails or refuses to surrender the license, they could be charged with a Class B Misdemeanor.

"BLOW & GO" / THE INTERLOCK DEVICE

Over the past decade or so, in-car ignition devices, commonly referred to as "blow and gos" have been developed and implemented by Texas courts to monitor and/or restrict the operation of certain person's cars. Texas law allows a court to order installation of an ignition interlock device on the vehicles of people who have been convicted of and placed on probation for DWI and other offenses, as a condition of bond and as a condition of granting an occupational driver's license. Texas law requires that courts must order installation of an Ignition Interlock Device on vehicles driven by someone arrested and charged with a second DWI as a condition of their bond.

There are several manufacturers of various ignition interlock devices. They are breath alcohol analyzers, which is connected to a vehicle's ignition system. Before the car is started, the driver must first blow a breath sample into the device, which then measures the alcohol concentration in the breath and prevents starting if the device detects a certain amount of alcohol in the driver's breath. A re-test is required once the car is started after a certain period of time has passed. All test results, starts, and "lock outs" are recorded on the device's internal hard drive and are downloaded each month the device is serviced. These records are made available to the courts for review, if requested. This has also become a little revenue source, as only certain companies are approve by the Courts and therefore profit from their being ordered in greater numbers.

WHAT'S THE PROBLEM?

There is a great amount of debate over the reliability of these types of machines. Prosecutors and law enforcement have taken the position that they are extremely accurate and therefore should be trusted completely. Defense attorneys, those accused, and others including scientists and researchers have differing views.

Breath analyzers (Breathalyzer, Intoxilyzer, Alcosensor, Alcoscan and BAC Datamaster are common brand names) don't actually test blood alcohol concentration (BAC), which requires the analysis of a blood sample. Instead, these machines estimate BAC indirectly, by and through an analysis of the person's breath, and then attempts to calculate what the BAC should be. A major problem with some of the machines used by law enforcement and especially these "blow & go" machines is that they not only detect the ethyl alcohol (or ethanol) found in alcoholic beverages, but also similar molecular structures found in other substances, thus indicating a presence of alcohol when there is none. According to the National Highway Traffic Safety Administration (NHTSA), even dieters and diabetics can have abnormally high acetone levels in their breath, which is just one of the substances referred to above. Other common substances have been reported to affect these machines, such as contact with and breathing the fumes of contact cement, paint, lacquers, paint removers, celluloid, gasoline, and cleaning fluids, residual alcohol from mouthwashes and other oral cleansers, blood or vomit, electrical interference from cell phones and police radios, tobacco smoke, dirt, moisture, even ambient temperature of the surrounding air, as well as the body temperature of the subject.

The long and the short of it is that they are machines that attempt to deduce and measure the alcohol amount in the blood by looking at the breath. You must decide what is reliable and what is or is not in your best interest.

PUBLIC INTOXICATION

Another area that may be cause for concern for those who drink is the ever-

The Student Body of Law

popular crime of public intoxication. This offense is utilized to great extent by the local authorities to control rowdiness and belligerent persons they may encounter during the course of their patrol. It is very often abused and gives the unethical officer an extremely subjective legal reason to arrest you if they wish. It is a very subjective decision by the officer whether you are committing the offense of Public Intoxication, so how you act and respond to an officer in your presence has a great deal of importance to your freedom at that time.

Let's say you have been out with some friends and you all decide to drop by the late-night diner for breakfast. You had a couple of pops at the bar earlier, but feel fine. The local police drop in for a cup of coffee and while they are there, for whatever reason, probably your friends' loud discussion about politics or religion, as well as the occasional curse word draws some attention. After settling up, your group leaves, no harm done. As you are walking down the sidewalk, the police officers stop you and ask for some ID. You produce your ID, but make a harmless comment or sarcastic remark that does not please the officer. He smells beer on your breath or asks "have you been drinking?". You reply "yes, a couple of beers." This is where things turn bad. Under Texas law, if the officer subjectively believes that you are intoxicated, not necessarily by the legal standard for DWI, but "to the degree that you may endanger yourself or another" (See Tex.Penal Code Sec. 49.02), the officer is legally authorized to arrest you and take you into custody for Public Intoxication, a Class C Misdemeanor. If you are under twenty-one, other potential problems lay in the Alcoholic Beverage Code. Nonetheless, you have to spend the night in a very unpleasant place: the local jail.

The same thing applies to parties, gatherings, concerts and festivals. Don't make the mistake of arguing with the officer or relying on what is or is not a "public place" under the law. For your own decision-making purposes, assume wherever you are, unless in your own home, you are in a public place and act accordingly.

DRUGS, THAT INCLUDES MARIJUANA

Drugs have been a right of passage and a part of America's youth, collegiate campuses, and the counter-culture since the 1960's. Various drugs rise and fall in popularity throughout the years, dependant on many different factors, such as availability, legality, costs, and general trendiness of their usage. The "drug war" was declared in the 1980's to confront the perceived problems associated with the drug trade with much stiffer sentences through the United States Sentencing Guidelines. The Texas Health and Safety Code deals with almost all of the major drug offense language, and by and large, the severity of the offense depends on what it is and how much is possessed, manufactured, or delivered.

MARIJUANA

Some of you may not actually realize that marijuana is illegal. Notwithstanding whether you think it should be legalized or not, right now in the state of Texas, it is a crime to possess a usable amount of marijuana. If it is less than four ounces, then it is considered a Misdemeanor (up to 2 oz. is a Class B Misdemeanor and 2-4 oz. is a Class A). It becomes a State Jail Felony if the amount is between 4 ounces and five pounds; a 3rd Degree Felony if the amount is over 5lbs. but under 50lbs.; and larger amounts escalate upwards to ninety-nine years as potential punishments. If the offense involves the manufacture, delivery, or intent to deliver any amount over ¼ oz., it's a felony.

CONTROLLED SUBSTANCES (Ecstasy, Cocaine, GHB, Mushrooms, etc...)

Possession of these substances and others found in the listed Penalty Groups 1-4 of the Texas Health and Safety Code are illegal without a valid prescription and the severity of the offense also depends on how much is possessed and in which penalty group they are listed. The general range is as follows but may vary depending on the actual substance possessed:

1. State Jail Felony - less than one gram (any detectable amount);
2. 3rd Degree Felony - 1 to 4 grams;
3. 2nd Degree Felony - 4 to 200 grams;
4. 1st Degree Felony; - 200 to 400 grams;
5. Over 400 grams - minimum of 10 years up to a life sentence.

The Student Body of Law

LSD - Lysergic Acid Diethylamide, more commonly referred to as "acid", is listed in its own "special" schedule due to the unusual way it is distributed (i.e. on little slips of paper or cards legally referred to as "abuse units", known on the street as a "dose" or "hit").

1. State Jail Felony — less than 20 abuse units;
2. 3rd Degree — 20-80 abuse units;
3. 2nd Degree Felony — 80 to 4,000 abuse units;
4. 1st Degree Felony; — 4,000 to 8,000 abuse units;
5. Over 8,000 abuse units — minimum of 15 years up to a life sentence.

STEROIDS

Anabolic steroids have been used for years by athletes to gain mass and muscle. The Drug War spawned new concerns about steroids in the late 1980's and ultimately resulted in new federal and state laws classifying many of these as controlled substances. Non-medical possession or sale of anabolic steroids is illegal and many of these substances are listed in the Texas Health and Safety Code. I'm certainly not going to preach about the health-related dangers of these substances or their reported side effects, but rather the legal consequences you may face if you decide to turn to their use or as a side business. The safest choice, both legally and medically is to stay clean and train drug-free, but if you decide otherwise, understand they are considered by law enforcement to be basically the same as any other street drug. The substances that have been outlawed are found in Penalty Group 3 and possession of these substances are classified as:

1. Class B Misdemeanor — less than 28 grams (any detectable amount);
2. 3rd Degree — 28 to 200 grams;
3. 2nd Degree Felony — 200 to 400 grams;
4. Over 400 grams — minimum of 5 years up to a life sentence.

MANUFACTURE OR DELIVERY

This raises the stakes a little and if you are dealing it generally raises the offense level one notch for the amount possessed, except the lowest levels remain the same and the higher end minimum prison sentences punishments are increased. A person commits this offense if they possess a controlled substance and knowingly manufacture, deliver, or possess with the intent to deliver a controlled substance. Intent to deliver may be proved by the way the drugs are packaged or by an amount that is not reasonable to believe would be for personal consumption.

DANGEROUS DRUGS

A "dangerous drug" is basically a prescription drug. Some popular drugs that usually fall into this category and are regularly prosecuted are Valium, Oxycontin, Darvocet, Haldol, Ritalin, etc. The legal definition means a device or a drug that is unsafe for self-medication, is not included in the Texas Controlled Substances Act, and includes a device or a drug that bears or is required to bear the legend: "Caution: federal law prohibits dispensing without prescription" or "Rx only" or another legend that complies with federal law; or "Caution: federal law restricts this drug to use by or on the order of a licensed veterinarian."

The safest choice, both legally and medically is to stay clean and train drug-free, but if you decide otherwise, understand they are considered by law enforcement to be basically the same as any other street drug.

Let's say you are complaining that your knee hurts from a game of touch football. One of your buddies offers some of his pain medicine from when he had his wisdom teeth pulled; he gives you a few pills and you take one and put the rest in the console of your car and forget about them. One night, months later, you're stopped for speeding and arrested for that outstanding ticket we talked about earlier. During the inventory search of your car they find those forgotten pills, BANG your under arrest for Possessing a Dangerous Drug, a Class A Misdemeanor. Your buddy's offer to give you the pills and the delivery is technically a State Jail Felony.

DRUG-FREE ZONES

Texas and other states have made certain places especially problematic for the possession of illegal drugs. Lets say you are living on campus and it's just another day in the life, when you roll out of the sack, let's say about 11am, flick on the tube, and spark up a bowl. You and your roommate are just hanging, when the knock on the door comes. You scramble around to hide the bong, spray some air freshener, and open the door to find the campus police standing there. After their initial interrogation, they enter your room and

The Student Body of Law

search it, finding the bong and your stash. BANG, you and your roommate are taken into custody. How much weed is there controls the severity of the charge, but more importantly, since you are in possession in a Drug Free Zone, the level of offense may be raised a level, making the charge much more severe than you ever thought possible.

The first question is, what is a Drug Free Zone? It encompasses lots of different areas, but mainly it includes:

1. Institutions of higher education, which means any public or private technical institute, junior college, senior college, or university, medical or dental unit, or other agency of higher education;
2. Playgrounds — any outdoor facility that is not on the premises of a school and that is intended for recreation; is open to the public; and contains three or more separate apparatus intended for the recreation of children, such as slides, swing sets, and teeterboards;
3. Schools — private or public elementary or secondary school or day-care centers;
4. Video arcades — any facility that is open to the public, including persons who are seventeen years of age or younger for the pri mary use of pinball or video machines with at least three pinball or video machines;
5. Youth centers — any recreational facility or gymnasium that is intended primarily for use by persons who are seventeen years of age or younger and regularly provides athletic, civic, or cultural activities;
6. Public Swimming Pools;
7. School Busses; and
8. Areas within 1,000 feet of premises owned, rented, or leased by an institution of higher learning, the premises of a public or private youth center, or a playground; or within 300 feet of the premises of a public swimming pool or video arcade facility are specifically included as Drug Free Zones.

Any manufacture, delivery, or intent to deliver a controlled substance in a Drug Free Zone is punishable as a felony and generally raises the level of offense by one level upwards. Mere possession of felony amounts of controlled substances in Drug Free Zones, except the State Jail Felony amounts will also raise the level of offense, as well as raise the minimum prison sentences for the higher levels.

Next time you think about sparking one up at the secluded playground or any other place that you think may be a Drug Free Zone remember the penalties go up if you're caught in those places.

DRUG PARAPHERNALIA

Possession of a bong, pipe, dugout, or whatever you're thinking about is a Class C Misdemeanor for a first time offense; a second offense is a Class A; or if you tried to give the paraphernalia to someone under eighteen; or gave it to someone who was going to use it to grow/manufacture/deliver/etc. illegal drugs, it is a State Jail Felony.

DRUG TESTING

This has not only become a very controversial subject, but has become prevalent in our society. Drug testing has become a regular course of policy in the workplace for new hires and continued employment, as well as in some school systems. Millions of citizens are required to submit to drug tests and the constitutionality of these policies and their violation of their 4th and 5th Amendment rights under the United States Constitution continue to be debated and litigated, but they are becoming more and more prevalent. It has been forecasted that if allowed, drug testing could reach into the admission and attendance process of some colleges. The practice of masking or trying to fool the tests has become big business and products claiming to beat the test are advertised everywhere from health food stores to the Internet. This book is not intended to either advocate or denounce such practices, nor is it to discuss the reliability of the products, but rather address legalities in Texas.

In Texas there is actually a law that makes it a crime to falsify drug test results. A person commits an offense if the person knowingly or intentionally uses, possesses with intent to use, manufactures, or delivers any substance or device designed to falsify drug test results.

GIRLS
HOW OLD IS OLD ENOUGH?

In Texas, once a young woman or young man turns seventeen years old, she/he is no longer considered a "child" as defined by the Texas Penal Code, and is considered to be of an age to lawfully engage in consensual sex with whomever she/he desires, except "deviant sexual intercourse" with a person

The Student Body of Law

of the same sex, and we'll revisit that in the SEXUAL CURIOSITY section. If she is under seventeen, she is considered a child and the person who engages in even consensual sexual conduct with the young woman may be exposed to criminal charges and/or prosecution, with certain exception(s). If the girl is under age seventeen, any consensual sexual conduct and/or exposure with a person that is more than three years older is unlawful. Therefore, if you are about to engage in consensual sexual acts with a person and that person is between fourteen and seventeen and you are more than three years older than that person, you better think twice and consider either waiting until that person turns seventeen or find another date. A person who decides to engage in such conduct with someone between the ages fourteen and seventeen and is more than three years older may expose themselves to a charge of Sexual Assault, which is a Second Degree Felony and can be prosecuted for such an offense for up to ten years after the "victim" turns eighteen years old. One other reminder, whether or not she told you she was seventeen or she's been with everyone else, it doesn't matter when it comes down to whether you may be arrested, charged, and convicted. If that person is below the age of fourteen it is an Aggravated crime and is the First Degree Felony of Aggravated Sexual Assault. Their sexual promiscuity is irrelevant to the charges.

BEAD-BAITING

While Joe and the guys were in New Orleans for Mardi Gras, they enjoyed the "bead baiting" of the women, so the next year, Joe and the boys bring this tradition home to Spring Break. From the balcony of their hotel room overlooking the South Padre Island beach, the boys are producing their own video of the girls going wild below by throwing them beads for their effort. Unfortunately, the local cops on Padre Island don't look the other way like in New Orleans and BANG the girls are busted for Indecent Exposure. Unfortunately, one of the girls Joe was coaxing into "exposing herself," turns out to be sixteen. BANG, Joe and the boys are arrested for the 2nd Degree Felony of

Sexual Performance of a Child.

Although this crime is intended to prevent the exploitation of underage kids — typically child pornography or other live performances where children are typically used or exhibited — it also makes it against the law to induce a child younger than eighteen to engage in sexual conduct or a sexual performance and therefore easy to see a situation where a zealous local DA may charge Joe and the guys with this offense. What has happened below Joe's hotel balcony is sexual conduct, because sexual conduct is defined as any sexual contact, actual, or simulated sexual intercourse, deviant sexual intercourse, sexual beastiality, masturbation, sado-masochistic behavior, or lewd exhibition of the genitals, the anus, or any portion of the female breast below the top of the areola.

"DEAD FISH"

Lets say Joe has been out at the local fraternity party and he meets a girl, has some drinks, dancing, lots of talking and laughter, more drinks, they really hit it off, but she has had a little too much to drink or even may be under the influence of a drug (prescription or otherwise). She and Joe are having a good time, mugging down in the corner and getting pretty hardcore. During the evening, Joe has even had the opportunity to see her license and his

Never put yourself in a position where there is any question of whether or not the person with whom you are engaging in any sexual conduct agrees to do so voluntarily.

concerns raised by the above section are put to rest. Joe offers to make sure she gets home safely, but when they get there, she asks Joe in. She turns on the TV and while sitting on the couch, they start kissing, things progress, and she even takes her shirt and jeans off, but then she proceeds to pass out. Not knowing what to do, Joe decides to go on without her and engages in sexual conduct with her, even though she is passed out. Under the Sexual Assault provision of the Texas Penal Code, it is considered an offense if the person has not consented AND the other person knows that she is unconscious or physically unable to resist. If you find yourself in Joe's shoes, be a gentleman, make her comfortable, cover her up, lock the door, and go home. Call her the next morning or leave her a nice note with your number.

Other legal ramifications may arise if you happen to provide your sexual

The Student Body of Law

partner with some popular forms of drugs such as ecstasy, GHB, rohypnol, ketamine, and others, especially if they aren't aware of your little practical joke. It's no joke and raises the offense to Aggravated status.

NO MEANS NO

One last word on this topic that hopefully goes without saying, "NO MEANS NO". Never put yourself in a position where there is any question of whether or not the person with whom you are engaging in any sexual conduct agrees to do so voluntarily. Any hint of conduct without consent, remorse, or guilt after the fact is precarious ground that can easily result in charges being accepted by the local District Attorney. Regret, embarrassment, and humiliation have all been common motivations for false allegations the next morning, and nothing will totally prevent your being accused of something criminal. Remember that taking advantage, coercing, or humiliating someone can all approach the line that can easily be interpreted as being without consent. If you try to conduct yourself as a gentleman, you will most likely avoid any allegation of misconduct and have all the fun in the world.

SOLICITATION OF A MINOR

So you have stumbled into a chat room and on the other end is someone that claims to be fourteen years old and you begin to chat. The chat turns sexual and some really provocative suggestions are made. Be careful. Even if you are just joking around, this can be taken as very serious. This has become a popular undercover operation of the government and may very well be a sting. You may very well be chatting with a law enforcement agent that is setting you up for a fall, even if you're not serious about what you are saying.

Criminal Solicitation of a Minor is committed when and if:

1) You have intent that an offense be committed, and the person requests, commands, or attempts to induce a minor to engage in specific conduct that, under the circumstances surrounding the actor's conduct as the actor believes them to be, would constitute an offense or make the minor a party to the commission of an offense listed; or,
2) You have intent that an offense be committed, and the person by any means requests, commands, or attempts to induce a minor or another whom the person believes to be a minor to engage in spe-

cific conduct that, under the circumstances surrounding the actor's conduct as the actor believes them to be, would constitute an offense under one of those sections or would make the minor or other believed by the person to be a minor a party to the commission of an offense under one of those sections.

The scariest part of this type of offense is that it is not a defense that the person on the other end of the chat is not actually a minor, but only that the person accused believes that the person is a minor (under seventeen) and makes the wrong suggestion or comment. Joking around can get you into trouble, even if you didn't mean to, so be careful of what you're saying and to whom it is being said.

SEXUAL CURIOSITY, PRECOCIOUSNESS, & THE PUBLIC

We have talked about how old is old enough, whether someone can consent to sex or not, internet romance, and even ungentlemanly conduct, but let's talk about sex in general and all the avenues that it may lead us down. Texas has made it a crime for anyone to engage in deviant sexual intercourse with anyone. The definition of Deviant Sexual Intercourse in Texas is any contact between any part of the genitals of one person and the mouth or anus of another person; or the penetration of the genitals or the anus of another person with an object, including a finger (See Sec. 21.01 Tex. Penal Code). Under a strict interpretation of this law, oral sex is considered to be deviant sexual conduct, but not illegal in and of itself, unless done so in conjunction with certain other circumstances.

It's a nice afternoon and Joe decides to go to the park with his girlfriend. They find a nice out-of-the-way spot amongst the trees, have a couple of beers, a nice picnic, and Joe's girlfriend starts to get a little more amorous. Joe and his girl both undress each other and roll around in the grass having sex in various ways and means. Two kids wander out of the nearby woods and witness Joe's sexual prowess, not to mention full frontal nudity. The kids, after gawking, go immediately to inform their parents on the other side of the park, who in turn summon the park police. BANG, no pun intended, Joe and his love may be subject to arrest and prosecution for several different offenses, such as: Public Lewdness, Indecent Exposure, and possibly even Indecency With a Child.

Public Lewdness is when one engages in an act of sexual intercourse,

The Student Body of Law

deviant sexual intercourse, an act of sexual contact, or an act involving contact between a person's mouth or genitals and the anus or genitals of an animal or fowl in a public place OR if not in a public place, is reckless about whether another is present and will be offended or alarmed by the behavior. This is a Class A Misdemeanor. This could include activities inside a person's own home or on their own property if it is done so in a reckless manner, i.e. can someone see it? Careful with the car and elevator sex as well, not to mention that goat.

Indecency with a Child is the most serious of these three potential problems for Joe and his nature-loving girl, albeit unlikely unless other more aggravating circumstances arose. A person commits Indecency with a Child when that person engages in sexual contact with a child (a person under age seventeen) either engages in either sexual contact (i.e. touching, groping, petting) OR exposes his anus or any part of his genitals with knowledge that the child is present, with the intent to arouse or gratify the sexual desire of any person (See PUBLIC NUDITY FOR FUN section).

COMPUTERS & HACKING
TEXAS COMPUTER CRIMES

Our old friend Joe is surfing the Internet one afternoon while sitting around the dorm room. Schmedley the geek from down the hall wanders by and they begin to talk computers. The subject of hacking comes up and Schmedley jumps on Joe's computer and quickly hacks into the university mainframe and looks around. BANG, they have committed the offense of Breach of Computer Security.

Texas law makes it a crime to knowingly access another person's computer, computer network, or computer system without the effective consent of the owner. Originally, it was required that the person, breach a computer security system in order to commit the offense. This requirement has since been removed by the legislature. "Effective consent" basically means permission to access the internal workings, files, programs, etc. of a computer or a network and such access is always without "effective consent" if it is without the knowledge of the owner of the computer or network. The key to this offense is the broad definition of the term "access." It not only includes altering data or computer software in the computer, but also just making use of the computer, even if there is absolutely no damage or alterations to the information, files, data or programs. Merely getting in and snooping around constitutes a crime.

Another aspect of this type of crime is that it includes not only unauthorized use, but also authorized use for an unauthorized purpose.

Joe has recently secured gainful employment in the school's data entry department, entering information and inventory information. One afternoon, he decides to browse the other files, which includes student files and grades, BANG. Joe has accessed files and information that he does not have authorization or effective consent to look at, much less to alter last semester's grades.

While working for the university, Joe has been given access to passwords to the university's computer network, which he quickly gives to Schmedley, the geek down the hall. BANG, he has again committed an offense by his unauthorized distribution of this type of information and even includes identifying codes, PIN numbers, debit card numbers, bank account numbers, and any other "confidential information about a computer security system."

Joe has committed a Class B Misdemeanor, but his crime may be elevated to a Class A Misdemeanor if there is any intent to obtain a benefit or to defraud/harm another. If the value or benefit to Joe or the damage/loss suffered by the university exceeds $1,500, it's a State Jail Felony and a 3rd Degree Felony if over $20,000.

This is the primary statute used in state prosecutions, but other more specific protections exist for computers and data, including federal laws protecting Federal Government computers and those used in interstate commerce.

THE FEDS & COMPUTERS

The federal law is similar to the laws in Texas, but goes into a little more detail dealing with specific types of computers. The basic federal computer crimes are contained in 18 U.S.C. §1030, which specifically deal with unauthorized use of computers and the alteration and/or destruction of the records and data they contain. The severity of the offense depends on whether the computer hacked is a "Federal Interest Computer" or contains national security, financial or credit information, or uses more than two computers in more than one state, which is almost always the case. A rudimentary overview of this area of law is that a person commits an offense if they: 1) obtain protected information from a computer concerning national defense, foreign relations, Atomic Energy, financial or credit transactions; 2) access a computer used exclusively by the Federal government, or information on a computer used by the Federal Government that adversely affects the Government's use; or is owned by the Federal Government, including a "Federal Interest Computer" with intent to commit fraud; 3) use a computer in interstate commerce, to transmit a program or command which damages, interrupts or prevents the use of a computer system or network; 4) traffic or otherwise distributes computer passwords for Federal Government Computers or in interstate commerce with the intent to defraud. Criminal penalties range from a fine of up to $100,000 and up to one year in prison, up to twenty years in a federal prison depending on the particular offense, amount of damage/fraud, and a person's criminal history.

As you can see, Texas and federal law are relatively parallel and may be prosecuted by either state or federal prosecutors, however, the Feds usually prosecute the more serious crimes and each usually investigates and prosecutes those crimes that their own investigative agencies have investigated (FBI, CIA, Secret Service are Feds). Nonetheless, no matter who investigates or prosecutes, there are certain instances that may be prosecuted in both state and federal courts for the same activity, notwithstanding traditional notions of double jeopardy.

PORN AND THE INTERNET

You are surfing the net and stumble upon images of some home-made photos of what appears to be the local high school cheerleading squad, posing in some explicit and compromising positions. As a prank, you send them to everyone in your address book and the images are saved on your hard-drive. This may very well be considered child pornography. Does that mean that the FBI is watching or about to bust through the door? Probably not, but as internet privacy issues continue to be contested, only your imagination can fathom the future developments of the internet and related technologies.

Under federal sentencing guidelines, even the mere possession of child pornography is punishable by two to ten years in a federal penitentiary, while the trafficking or exchange of child porn is punishable by up to thirty years in federal prison. Investigations have recently revealed adults were routinely working with computers to lure minors into engaging in sexually explicit activity, either with frontal nudity or by interacting with other minors, adults, and animals.

The Supreme Court has determined that images of minors, which appear to have the "intent to arouse" constitute child pornography. Even the mere exchange of photos over the internet may constitute trafficking and subject private parties to suspicion and potentially harsh penalties.

While adult pornography on the internet is subject to First Amendment protections, child pornography holds no such rights, and all state laws deem the trafficking of child porn images a felony. Possession of child pornography, on the other hand, is in many states classified as a misdemeanor. What is or is not child pornography will continue to be subject to legal scrutiny, judicial review, and change in the future and will continue to be the subject of criminal investigations and subsequent prosecutions as the proliferation of these images are accessed through the internet. What makes this particular area of law so scary is that the viewer or possessor of these images does not have to know that the persons depicted are actually children, but they can merely appear to be a minor. If it sounds like its difficult to determine exactly what is or is not against the law, that's because it is, for the most part. Many different scenarios have already arisen and many more will follow.

Internet service providers are not required by law to police their own networks, with the result being many pornography web sites operate with impunity until complaints are lodged with the Department of Justice or local law enforcement.

What should you do to protect yourself? If you do stumble upon these types of images or are suspicious, your best bet is to make sure you don't download them or send them to others. To the best of your computer skills, destroy those images and stay away from those sites that promote such images.

An area of concern dealing with communications through the internet and privacy concerns continue to be addressed in the courts, but it is safe to assume that your communications over the internet are not necessarily confidential and someone may very well either be watching, intercepting, or keeping a record of your communications. They can not only be intercepted, but may be interpreted without the benefit of the whole truth or taken out of context. Jokes, pranks, and fantasy can be interpreted in many different ways, so use some restraint when communicating over the internet to ensure that such words are not taken out of context or interpreted to your detriment.

HAZING

What is Hazing? The short answer is almost everything that used to be fun.

The Student Body of Law

But seriously, this has become a problem on college campuses, mainly in the Greek community, but is no longer limited to fraternities and sororities. Other campus organizations have been sanctioned and prosecuted as well. What were once harmless rituals and rites of passage have evolved into acts of brutality and unaccepted conduct causing both physical and emotional damage. Because of this escalation of severity, the criminal law has stepped in.

The Long Answer: Hazing is any intentional, knowing, or reckless act, occurring on or off the campus, directed against a student, that endangers the mental or physical health or safety of a student for the purpose of pledging, being initiated into, affiliating with, holding office in, or maintaining membership in an organization. Examples include:

1. Physical Brutality (i.e. whipping, beating, striking, branding, electronic shocking, placing of a harmful substance on the body, trading swats, fights, boxing matches, etc.);
2. Physical Activity (i.e. sleep deprivation, exercise, exposure to the elements, confinement in a small space, kidnapping, drops, rides, etc.);
3. Consumption of a food, liquid, alcoholic beverage, liquor, drug or other substance;
4. Activity that intimidates or threatens the student with ostracism;
5. Activity that subjects the student to extreme mental stress, shame, humiliation, degradation or discourages the student from entering or remaining registered in an educational institution, or that may reasonably be expected to cause a student to leave the organization or the institution rather than submit to acts described in this subdivision (i.e. nudity, individual interrogation, lineups, personal servitude, demeaning names & nicknames, yelling or screaming); and
6. Activity that induces, causes, or requires the student to perform a duty or task that involves a violation of the Penal Code.

Anyone connected with hazing, from those who directly engage in the activity to those who encourage, solicit, direct, aid or attempt to aid in the hazing activity, or recklessly permit the hazing; or even knows of a past specific act of hazing or one that is planned and knowingly fails to report that knowledge in writing to the dean of students or other appropriate official of the institution are all susceptible to the law. Even the organization may be fined if it condones or encourages the hazing. The fact that the pledge consented is not a defense. Hazing is a Class B misdemeanor, Class A if it results in bodily injury, and a felony if it results in death.

HOAXES & PRACTICAL JOKES

Dorm Life. Who hasn't played some type of practical joke on a fellow roommate or dorm mate? It's more important to try to have some harmless fun, and not take this activity to the degree that someone might actually get hurt.

Joe is hanging around the dorm with his roommate when the most obnoxious and crude guy in the dorm comes home. He goes into his room and as a joke, Joe "pennies" his door closed. For those who don't know what this is, it is done by jamming a small stack of pennies, or other coins, in the space between the door and the jam to wedge the door shut so the occupant cannot open the door. Sounds like some good old fashioned fun, but Joe forgets about the door and the guy misses a final the next morning or there is a fire in the dorm that night and he can't escape. Forget about possibly being charged with unlawful restraint, the death will undoubtedly create some very unpleasant and unexpected legal problems, not to mention the ethical problems of causing this guy's death. Granted, this is an extreme scenario, but strange and unexpected things do happen.

Dry Ice Bomb. One afternoon Joe and some buddies are bored and try a little experiment in the dorm parking lot. Joe's geeky chemistry lab partner takes an empty 2-liter coke bottle, builds up the pressure in it, and caps it off. Joe and the guys stand back as the pressure builds and then, BANG, it explodes, causing people to spill out of the dorms; someone even calls the cops. Someone may be taken into custody for a Class A Misdemeanor of Prohibited Weapon, unless the cops either have a sense of humor themselves or Joe can convince them they were actually testing the laws of physics.

An "explosive weapon", which is a Prohibited Weapon and therefore unlawful to possess, manufacture, transport, repair or sell is defined as "any explosive or incendiary bomb grenade, rocket, or mine, that is designed, made, or adapted for the purpose of inflicting serious bodily injury, death, or substantial property damage, or for the principle purpose of causing such a loud report as to cause undue public alarm or terror, and included a device designed, made, or adapted for delivery or shooting an explosive weapon." Whether or not the "dry ice bomb" qualifies will be up to the local cops and DA to decide.

The Student Body of Law

Potato Guns. These contraptions do not fit exactly into any illegal category, but it could be argued that they very well qualify as a firearm in that they "expel a projectile through a barrel by using the energy generated by an explosion", which is the basic definition of a firearm in Texas. Certainly, if these are used in a way that causes injury or serious bodily injury they could be deadly weapons under Texas law. Be careful, these things can cause serious injury to those trying to build or use the homemade tater cannons.

Fun with Laser Pointers. One of Joe's buddies, Schmedley has gotten his hands on a laser poiner. You know, one of those little pen-like pointers used for presentations, which you usually may see at the movies when some annoying butthead, like Joe, continually points it at the screen. It becomes somewhat of a joke with the guys to use it for pranks at lectures, graduation ceremonies and other annoying occasions. One evening as they are on the way to a movie, Joe drives by a university police officer working traffic control and Schmedley, sitting in the back, points it at the officer. BANG, the car is stopped and someone is either arrested or ticketed for a Class C Misdemeanor, not to mention all the other things that go along with being stopped, like questioning, IDs run for warrants, and the car searched. It is unlawful to "direct a light from a laser pointer at a uniformed safety officer, including a peace officer, security guard, firefighter, emergency medical service worker, or other uniformed municipal, state, or federal officer.

It's Just a Joke, Man! Just like drugs, fake drugs can get you into hot water. Hoaxs, pranks, and practical jokes are fun, but if your not careful in their planning, they can get the authorities involved. What makes this illegal is not only the intent, but the harm or alarm to those subjected to the joke. For example, if the hoax bomb Joe created is intended to make someone believe it is actually a bomb or to cause alarm or reaction of any type of government official that deals with emergency situations OR when Joe pennied the guy's dorm room door shut (think about the term illegal restraint) OR when you douse the same guy with five gallons of pudding as he leaves for a date, think assault and/or criminal mischief.

PUBLIC NUDITY FOR FUN

Flashing, Streaking & Just Taking a Leak. Indecent Exposure is committed when a person exposes his/her anus or any part of his genitals with intent to arouse or gratify the sexual desire of any person and is reckless about whether another person is present who will be offended or alarmed by the act. This is a Class B Misdemeanor.

The classic situation is the behavior exhibited by numerous young women at Mardi Gras, or the predilection of many young men to bear their backside, the time honored tradition of the "pressed ham" on the car window, or even the dated '70's act of streaking. Although not calculated to "gratify the sexual desire of anyone", these crimes are all regularly prosecuted in the courts throughout Texas and if not taken seriously and vigorously defended, the charges could have life long effects. See SEX CRIMES & SEX OFFENDER REGISTRATION section for more details.

Let's say Joe is walking down the street. It's late, Joe's been walking for awhile and still has a ways to go, but nature calls and Joe's gotta go. Joe walks behind a dumpster, hopefully out of view, unzips and relief pours over him. All of a sudden a police cruiser's spot-light illuminates the entire area as Joe's essential human act of urination takes center stage. BANG, Joe's probably under arrest for Indecent Exposure. Joe really hasn't learned his lesson and does exactly the same thing a year or two later. If convicted a second time, guess what he is? That's right. A sex offender and now has a "reportable conviction". See SEX CRIMES & SEX OFFENDER REGISTRATION section for more details.

GAMBLING

The Friendly Wager. Let's say you lay a 20-spot on the Giants giving $5\frac{1}{2}$, with some guy in Science Lab. Gambling is generally considered an illegal activity, but gambling, in and of itself, is not illegal. What makes it illegal is when someone other than the person betting receives some of the money or if it was in public and if the odds are not the same for everyone. Simply put, since the bet is only between you two, it's not illegal. Same goes for the football squares and the March Madness brackets — nobody is making money without some risk.

Bookies. The real area of illegal gambling that you may actually bump into is with a bookie. It is a Class A Misdemeanor to operate or participate in the earnings of a gambling place that engages in bookmaking; sells chances or promotes a lottery (better known as "the numbers"), including communicating information as to bets, betting odds, or changes in betting odds. Historically, college campuses always have some entrepreneurs, mathematics students, or computer geeks that establish their own bookmaking system. Years ago, the University of Texas was home to one of the largest

The Student Body of Law

student/campus betting syndicates ever, which was ultimately busted and its administrators prosecuted.

How Bookies Work. A bookmaker's posted odds are not intended to be predictions. The purpose of odds is to make sure the bookmaker gets enough action on both sides of a bet to make sure that they win no matter what happens. If the betting public's opinion is not reasonably balanced, a disproportionate amount of money would be wagered on one side of a game, thus forcing the bookmaker to gamble, and bookmakers are not in the business to actually gamble. Really? Absolutely not! The bookie's role, strictly speaking, is to act as a broker, much like a stockbroker. His job is to "hold the money" and to charge a fee for that service. This is the fee that the bookie charges even if the bet ends up even. It is this particular transaction that makes gambling through the bookie illegal, because the bookie will make money whatever the outcome.

Bookies come in all shapes and sizes and can turn out to be some very unpleasant people, especially when you lose and owe them money. If you really have to have action on the game, I suggest opening an account on-line with any number of legitimate gambling sites or keep the stakes low and gamble amongst friends with friendly wager stakes.

The Weekly Poker Game & Texas Hold'Em. The weekly poker game at Joe's buddy's apartment or even the recently popular Texas Hold'em tournaments are not illegal, unless the house takes a cut as their fee. Local authorities around the state have taken the position that such tournaments held in public places, such as bars, clubs and other similar places, especially if they have licenses to sell alcohol, cannot be legally held. It seems that the public nature can be interpreted as the illegal element of this violation. Nonetheless, such a tournament held in a private home or other privately controlled environment that doesn't directly benefit financially from the card tournament is legal.

Card houses still exist and are there for two main reasons: 1) to provide professional card players a venue and access to novice players (you the pigeon) and their money; and 2) to take your money for the privilege of throwing you to the wolves. The fairest and safest game, if there is one, is at a legitimate casino, if there is one, not in the back rooms. Remember, if you sit down at the table and don't know who the sucker is, it's YOU.

THE GREAT OUTDOORS

Hunting & Fishing. First off, it is against the law to hunt or fish on privately owned lands or waters without the permission of the owner or the owner's agent. Check out the TRESPASSING section of Chapter 8.

Everyone that's hunting, fishing, or trapping must carry on their person and have available for inspection a valid license and any applicable stamps or permits unless the person is exempt from license, stamp, or permit requirements. Anyone seventeen or older must also carry on their person a driver's license or personal identification certificate issued by the Texas DPS and if not from Texas, they must have the same sort of ID issued by a home state or country.

Unless in compliance with the laws of Texas and properly licensed, it is unlawful to take, attempt to take, or possess wildlife resources within a protected length limit, in greater numbers, by other means, or at any time or place. Basically, know the size, bag limits, and season and you'll be okay, otherwise you better find out before you go. You can check out all the regulations at the Texas Department of Parks and Wildlife website at www.tpwd.state.tx.us or call them at: (800) 792-1112 or (512) 389-4800.

A hunter must always make a reasonable effort to retrieve all wounded game birds and animals, must kill them immediately, and count them against your legal bag limit. Careful though, you can't pursue a wounded animal across someone else's property line without their consent, otherwise you run the risk of being arrested for criminal trespass. You must also keep all edible portions of a game bird or animal, or fish in an edible condition.

Always know where you are and be careful where you shoot because it is against the law to discharge a firearm on or across a public road.

On the flip side, anyone that harasses a hunter, trapper, or fisherman, if convicted, may be punishable by a fine of $200 to $2000 and/or 180 days in jail under the Sportsmen's Rights Act.

You are not required to have a fishing license to fish in private waters in Texas; but, not so if your fishing public water on private property. It is an offense to fish from the deck or road surface of any bridge or causeway on a road maintained by the Texas Dept. of Transportation, but it's okay to fish public waters from a highway right of way or underneath a highway bridge, depending on whether or not the water is private. Keep reading. It may or may not help you to understand this confusing area of law.

Game Wardens. A game warden who observes a person engaged in an activity governed by the Texas Parks and Wildlife Code or reasonably believes that a person is or has been engaged in such an activity has the right to

The Student Body of Law

inspect: 1) any license, permit, tag, or other document issued by the department and required by the Texas Parks and Wildlife Code of a person hunting or catching wildlife resources; 2) any device that may be used to hunt or catch a wildlife resource; 3) any wildlife resource in the person's possession; and 4) the contents of any container or receptacle that is commonly used to store or conceal a wildlife resource. A game warden or other peace officer may also inspect any wildlife resource that has been taken by a person and is in plain view, but cannot otherwise search a person's residence or temporary residence beyond the constitutional restrictions discussed earlier.

"Residence" means a person's principal or ordinary home or dwelling place and "temporary residence" means a place where a person temporarily dwells or seeks shelter and includes: hunting clubs or lodges; cabins; tents; hotel and motel rooms; and boardinghouse rooms used during a hunting trip, but NOT a hunting blind.

Rivers & Lakes. The State of Texas owns the water in every lake and natural stream, as well as the fish that live there, but the public does not have the right to fish or boat in private lakes or streams. This gets really complicated, especially since Texas land titles originated with Spanish or Mexican land grants, which did not distinguish between public and private streams on the basis of navigability.

Generally, a body of water, whether a stream, creek, river or lake is accessible to the public if it is either "navigable in fact," or "navigable by statute." What makes a stream "navigable in fact" is unclear, but is generally considered to be waters in their natural state that are useful to the public for a considerable portion of the year. A stream is "navigable by statute" if it retains an average width of thirty feet and includes the entire streambed, not just the area covered by water on a given day. A navigable stream may even be completely dry part of the year, but still remains public regardless of the water level on any given day. The entire streambed is public, but what is exactly included in the streambed is also a bit fuzzy. The streambed can best be described as the portion of soil which is alternately covered and left bare as the supply of water fluctuates, which contains the stream at its average and mean stage during an entire year. It has also been described as the land between the "gradient boundary" on each bank. Got it?

You may boat, canoe, tube, swim, float, walk, wade, picnic, fish (with a license), even camp in public water, but must be confined to the waters of the lake or stream and the streambed. You do not have the right to cross private property to get to or from the public water which would constitute criminal trespass, if the other elements of the offense are present. Portage is sometimes necessary to scout a dangerous condition or safe route or to avoid it altogether by walking around. Anytime you portage, you may be flirting with criminal trespass and the defense of necessity. Your best bet is to minimize your intrusion on anyone's land unless absolutely necessary for safety.

Since the public has a general right to walk and boat in a public stream or lake, a landowner has no right to erect or maintain a fence that interferes with those lawful activities, in fact it is a crime to obstruct a public waterway to make passage impossible, unreasonably inconvenient, or hazardous. A person who interferes with a lawful boater may be committing the crime of obstructing a waterway and/or harassment, just as a boater who unreasonably obstructs access to or from a dock or boat slip may also be guilty of obstructing a waterway.

The State of Texas extends three marine leagues (nine nautical miles, or 10.359 statute miles) into the Gulf of Mexico from the coastline and owns the water, the beds, and shores of the Gulf of Mexico, and the arms of the gulf, including all land, which is covered by the gulf and the arms of the gulf either at low tide or high tide. The public has a general right to boat and fish in the waters of the Gulf of Mexico within Texas, including all of its bays and arms. Even though some private land along the coast is covered intermittently or continuously by tide waters due to some man-made condition, the general rule is "if you can float it you can boat it," even if the land beneath the waters may be privately owned. As for wade fisherman in these areas, it is unclear if they may be trespassing.

Lastly, it is now a crime to drive a motor vehicle in the bed of a navigable freshwater stream, unless approved by a local river access plan established by a city, county, or river authority, but this does not apply to the Red and Canadian rivers.

Camping & Fires

Joe and his buddies decide to head out for a weekend of camping, male bonding, and drinking in the woods. They head to the local state park, pick out a nice area where they set-up camp, crank the jam box, and start downing the beers. Some also gather wood for the raging fire that has been lit near the campsite.

Whether in a private camping area or in one of the many Texas state

The Student Body of Law

parks, there are probably rules that you are going to have to follow. Generally, camping is defined as: occupying a designated camping facility; or erecting a tent, or arranging bedding, or both, for the purpose of, or in such a manner as will permit, remaining overnight; or use of a trailer, camper, or other vehicle for the purpose of sleeping during night time hours. Joe's outdoor party is probably going to experience some problems from the local park ranger, most notably the regulations that protect the other campers in the park from noise disturbances and the fire.

It is an offense to disturb other persons in sleeping quarters or in campgrounds between the hours of 10 p.m. and 6 am; and to cause, create, or contribute to any noise which is broadcast, or caused to be broadcast, into sleeping quarters or campgrounds, or which emits sound beyond the person's immediate campsite, between the hours of 10 p.m. and 6 a.m., whether by shouting or singing, by using a radio, phonograph, television, or musical instrument, or by operating mechanical or electronic equipment; to use electronic equipment, including electrical speakers, at a volume which emits sound beyond the immediate individual camp or picnic site at any time without specific permission of the director; or by creating a disturbance by causing excessive noise by any mean.

It is also an offense to light, build, or maintain a fire within a state park except in a facility or device provided, maintained, or designated for such purposes, such as campsite grills, fire rings, or fireplaces, or to build fires when an extreme fire hazard has been posted. When dry conditions warrant, county judges and/or county commissioners regularly implement fire bans. Look for signs or ask at the gate for specific campfire information. Some primitive sites have fire rings and some beach sites allow ground fires on sandy areas if approved by the park manager, but firewood may not be gathered unless authorized by the park manager.

BOATS AND JET SKIS

This section is included just in case some of you are interested in boating, including jet skis. All classes of jet skis are considered "personal water craft" and the laws apply to them, just like boats, but are referred to as PWCs.

So Joe and the boys are headed to the lake with dad's ski boat for a day of skiing and outdoor fun in the sun. They load up the skis and wake boards, ice down the cool beverages for the day, and head to Lake Travis. They spend several hours skiing and drinking beer, catching some rays, and having a great time. Even the girls that managed to come along are having fun. As they are tooling around headed to Devil's Cove for a rest and some company, the local water cops pull up and ask to inspect the boat, and question the driver about his paperwork and his alcohol consumption. BANG, the boys are in trouble. The driver is seventeen, intoxicated, and there are several violations on the boat, namely not enough life jackets and too many people on the boat. Never overfill the boat capacity. The capacity plate is usually near the operator's position or on the boat's transom and will tell you what the maximum weight capacity or maximum number of people that the boat can safely carry.

The DWI laws are basically the same for boats as they are for other vehicles, so take a look at the DWI section in Chapter 6 for a full explanation. All marine safety enforcement officers, law enforcement, and game wardens have the authority to enforce all boating laws, including the right to stop and board boats to check for compliance with federal and state laws. The U.S. Coast Guard has enforcement authority on federally controlled waters.

You must have a Texas Certificate of Number (registration) and a validation decal to legally operate your boat on Texas' public waters. The only exceptions are for sailboats under fourteen feet in length and non-motorized boats such as canoes, kayaks, punts, rowboats, and rubber rafts. The certificate of number and decal must also be prominently displayed on the boat.

The rest of this particular area is confusing and a bit tedious, because Texas is in the midst of requiring all underage boaters to have completed a boater education course before they operate a boat or PWC. Especially since most of you reading this are somewhere around the cutoff age, it gets even more confusing. Read it carefully and hopefully it will make sense.

MANDATORY BOATER EDUCATION

Anyone born after August 31, 1984 is legally required to pass a boater education course before they can legally operate: 1) A boat or PWC powered by a motor of ten horsepower or more; or, 2) A sailboat over fourteen feet in length. These persons must carry with them on the boat or PWC: 1) A photographic identification, such as a driver's license; and, 2) A boater education certification card issued by Texas Parks & Wildlife Department. Those born after August 31, 1984, are exempted from the above if they: 1) Are eighteen or older; 2) licensed by the U.S. Coast Guard to serve as a master of a boat; 3) Operating the boat only on a private lake or pond; 4) Are accompanied on board by a person eighteen years of age or older who is exempt from this

The Student Body of Law

requirement; or 5) Are not a resident of Texas and have proof that they have passed a TPWD-approved boater education course in another state. The long and the short of it is that if you were born after August 31, 1984, and are under eighteen years of age, you must have passed a boater education course approved by Texas Parks & Wildlife to operate a boat or PWC powered by a motor of ten horsepower or more.

LEGALLY REQUIRED EQUIPMENT
LIFE PRESERVERS

There's a good reason they're called that. Probably the most important pieces of equipment that is required by law, as well as good sense, are life preservers and ski vests, otherwise known as "personal floatation devices" or PFDs. All boats must have at least one Type I, II, III or V personal flotation device that is U.S. Coast Guard-approved for each person on board. Children under thirteen must wear a U.S. Coast Guard-approved PFD while underway (not at anchor or moored or aground) in a boat of less than twenty-six feet in length. All boats sixteen feet or longer must have at least one Type IV U.S. Coast Guard-approved PFD on board and readily accessible, which means they don't have to be worn, just accessible. You must wear a PFD if riding a PWC or while skiing or otherwise being towed. There must also be a throwable floatation device on the boat. There are other specifications, but most-important is to have them, at least enough for everyone on the boat.

FIRE EXTINGUISHER

People forget about this one all the time, but it can be extremely important if there is a fire, and believe me, it happens more than you might think.

SOUND PRODUCING DEVICES

Boats less than 39.4 ft. (12 meters) in length, including PWCs, must have a whistle or horn or some other means to make an efficient sound signal. Longer boats must also have a bell. You should also be familiar with some of the common sound signals. If the visibility is restricted due to weather of fog: 1) One prolonged blast at intervals of not more than two minutes is the signal used by powerboats when underway; 2) One prolonged plus two short blasts at intervals of not more than two minutes is the signal used by sailboats under sail alone. In the case of warning other boats when coming around a sharp or blind corner or close quarters, use one prolonged blast as a warning signal. In the case of an emergency, to signal danger, or when you don't understand another boater's intentions, use five (or more) short, rapid blasts.

OTHER RULES FOR PWC

If equipped with a lanyard type engine the cutoff switch must be attached to the person, clothing, or PFD of the operator. It is illegal to: 1) Operate a PWC between sunset and sunrise; 2) Operate a PWC within fifty feet of another boat or PWC, a person, a stationary platform or a shoreline, except when maintaining headway speed; 3) Operate a PWC in a manner that requires the operator to swerve at the last possible moment to avoid collision; and 4) a PWC should not jump the wake of another boat recklessly or unnecessarily close to that boat.

BOATING AT NIGHT

Can't ski between one half hour after sunset until one half hour before sunrise and no PWCs between sunset and sunrise. Navigation lights are required and depends on the size of the boat.

WHEN UNDERWAY

Any boat, whether powered or not, must display red and green sidelights visible from at least one mile, and an all-round white light or both a masthead light and a sternlight, visible from at least two miles on a dark clear night and must be at least 3.3 ft. (1 meter) higher than the sidelights. An un-powered boat under 23 ft. can exhibit only a white light/lantern.

WHEN MOORED OR ANCHORED OFFSHORE

All boats are required to use an all-round white light whenever they are moored or anchored away from dock between sunset and sunrise.

CHAPTER SEVEN
Self-defense, Guns, and Weapons

Certainly, you can defend yourself, your girlfriend, your friend, or a stranger on the street, as well as your car, home, and other property as you see fit, but how and to what degree you do so lawfully is limited to the interpretation of the law and the facts in each situation. Texas has the reputation that our communities as well as juries allow a little more force than most. I will give it to you straight and simple so you can understand the basic laws. The most important distinction to understand and remember is that between force and deadly force.

SELF-DEFENSE
Use of Force • A person may use force against another, as well as the threat of force, or even actual confinement is justified when and to the degree he reasonably believes the force is immediately necessary to protect himself against the other's use or attempted use of unlawful force except: 1) in response to verbal provocation alone; 2) to resist an arrest or search by a peace officer, even if unlawful; 3) where the person consents to the exact force used or attempted by the other; 4) where the person provokes the other's use or attempted use of unlawful force (unless the actor abandons the encounter, or clearly communicates to the other his intent to do so reasonably believing he cannot safely abandon the encounter; and the other continues or attempts to use unlawful force against the actor; or 5) where a person seeks an explanation from or discussion with the another while carrying a weapon in violation of Sec. 46.02; or possessing or transporting a weapon in violation of Sec. 46.05.

The Incident • As Joe works his way through the crowd at the local club, some guy bumps into him spilling beer down the front of his shirt. Joe says "excuse me", while he responds with an expletive. Joe rears back and whacks him in the head with his beer bottle. BANG, the bouncers grab Joe, drag him through the club and hand him straight to the local cops standing at the front door. This jerk's bad manners do not justify Joe hitting him with his beer bottle. If he had made these comments while raising his hand to apparently hit Joe, then he can use force to attempt to prevent his striking Joe, basically getting the first shot.

"Let's step outside" • Instead of acting impulsively, Joe asks him outside to settle it, which they do. In this situation both may have consented to the force each uses on each other, but this is difficult to employ either at trial or when the cops drag them both off to jail for disturbing the peace or some other public order type of offense.

If both go outside and once the other guy sees Joe rip off his shirt and flex his underdeveloped physic, he says, "I don't want any of that," and turns to go back into the club, Joe's tackling him and wrestling him to the ground will be considered an assault. The cops will take Joe to jail, no matter what the jerk said inside the club.

The Arrest • The use of force to resist an arrest or search is justified only if: 1) before the person offers any resistance, the peace officer (or person acting at his direction) uses or attempts to use greater force than necessary to make the arrest or search; and 2) when and to the degree the person reasonably believes the force is immediately necessary to protect himself against the peace officer's (or other person's) use or attempted use of greater force than necessary.

As the bouncers hand Joe over to the cops and they try to handcuff him, he wriggles around and flails his arms, apparently unwilling to cooperate with the cops. In the mild melée outside, a cop falls and sprains his knee and Joe's hand flails and hits him in the eye. Both of these things cause him pain. BANG, an additional charge of either resisting arrest (misdemeanor) or assault on a peace officer (felony) are added to the assault on the jerk inside.

Threats • A threat to cause death or serious bodily injury by the production of a weapon or otherwise is generally justified, and as long as the actor's purpose is limited to creating an apprehension that he will use deadly force if necessary, does not constitute the use of deadly force.

Instead of Joe's response with the bottle to the jerk's head, Joe tells him to leave him alone or he'll mess him up. This is probably okay so long as his intent is only to create apprehension to effect his leaving him alone. If Joe's comments are not reasonable for the situation and the jerk's aggression, he may be subject to a Class C Misdemeanor Assault or a Terroristic Threat (Class B Misdemeanor)

The Student Body of Law

DEADLY FORCE

Self Defense • A person is justified in using deadly force against another if he would be justified in using force under Section 9.31 of the statute when and to the degree he reasonably believes that deadly force is immediately necessary to protect himself against the other's use or attempted use of unlawful deadly force, if a reasonable person in the same situation would have not retreated. The retreat requirement does not apply when someone has unlawfully entered your home. You can also use deadly force to prevent the imminent commission of aggravated kidnapping, murder, rape, or robbery.

The Dark Alley • You and Joe find yourselves outside the club after closing time and you both see the jerk and his buddies hanging around in the parking lot. As you walk towards your car, you see the jerk and his friends begin to walk in your direction. He has a baseball bat in his hand. You look around and realize that his friends have circled around and there is nowhere to go. Even if there was, you feel they would follow you. He continues towards Joe, and without thinking, Joe grabs an empty 40oz laying on the ground and whacks him in the head as he rushes towards him. You both then run off. Unfortunately for the jerk, the 40oz shattered and cut his jugular vein and he bled to death within minutes. Joe's actions appear reasonable under the circumstances and he will most likely avoid prosecution and/or conviction for the death.

Defense of Another Person • A person may use deadly force against an attacker to protect another person *if* he would be justified to use it to protect himself. He must also reasonably believe his intervention is immediately necessary to protect the other person from serious injury or death.

The Good Guy • As you and your buddies leave the bar at closing time, you see a struggle behind one of the cars. As you get closer, you hear a girl's voice say "no" and see that her shirt is torn and some guy is holding her down against the trunk of the car. You are justified in using force against the guy to protect her from injury. If it is reasonable that you think he is trying to rape or seriously injure her, then your actions in whacking him with a 2-by-4 in the head are probably justified as well.

Protecting Your Property • A person may use deadly force against another to protect his own property to the degree he reasonably believes the force is immediately necessary to prevent the other's imminent commission of arson, burglary, robbery, theft during the nighttime, or criminal mischief during the nighttime, and he reasonably believes that the property cannot be protected by any other means. This includes the use of deadly force to prevent the flight of someone after committing burglary, robbery, or theft during the nighttime, from escaping with the property he reasonably believes cannot be recovered by any other means; or, the use of force, other than deadly force, to protect or recover the property would expose him or another to a substantial risk of death or serious bodily injury. (Nighttime is defined as the period thirty minutes after sunset until thirty minutes before sunrise.)

The Burglar • Late one night you are awakened by the sound of someone breaking into your apartment. You get out of bed and grab your gun. As you peer around the corner, you see some guy grabbing your TV. You shoot the guy and he drops dead in your living room. Traditional thinking is this one is a no brainer. Even if you miss with the first shot and the burglar runs out the door with the TV, you are still justified in using your gun to try to stop him. The old adage that if you shoot 'em on the lawn, you better drag them in the house is not quite accurate. The critical factor is that the burglar is attempting to escape with the property; if you scare him off with the gunshot and he just runs off without anything, don't shoot, its probably not legally justified. A dead burglar on the lawn with a gunshot wound to the back will probably not escape serious scrutiny from the local DA and Grand Jury. That's not to say that it will get you indicted for murder, but Texas has seen its share of frontier justice. That's where the drag 'em in off the lawn adage comes from, but I don't recommend it.

The Pizza Guy • Late one night you hear someone banging on your front door, you get up, get your gun and go to the door. You ask who is there and the response is: "Open the damn door." You ask again and the response is louder: "You better open the damn door!" You then say, "I've got a gun, get away from my door or I'll shoot." The response from the other side is more expletives. You then fire a shot right through the door and you hear something that sounds like a person fall. You open the door and there sprawls Joe, the pizza guy, with a gaping wound to the head. Joe had the wrong apartment and thought you were refusing to open and pay for the pizza. You have some serious problems and will probably have the case sent to the Grand Jury to

The Student Body of Law

review your actions. Your mistake does not excuse your actions. The circumstances, Joe the pizza guy's actions, and your fear may affect how the matter is handled, but because of your actions, Joe the pizza guy is dead.

Use of Device to Protect Property • Sometimes, people have rigged deadly weapons to kill or maim a person who enters a house or land. Dorm rooms are notorious playpens for practical jokes and sometimes people rig devices that will inflict injury or even death to anyone that may unknowingly enter. If injury occurs in this sort of situation, the use of a device to protect land or tangible, movable property is only justified if: 1) the device is not designed to cause, or known by the actor to create a substantial risk of causing, death or serious bodily injury; and, 2) the device is reasonable under all the circumstances as the actor reasonably believes them to be when he installs the device. If you're thinking of this type of thing, maybe a dog or video camera would be a better solution to your problem.

To Protect Someone Else's Property • A person may use force or deadly force against another to protect the property of a third person if he reasonably believes he would be justified to use similar force to protect his own property, and he reasonably believes that there existed an attempt or actual commission of the crime of theft or criminal mischief. This applies also if the person reasonably believes that the third person has requested his protection of property; or he has a legal duty to protect the property; or the third person whose property he is protecting is his spouse, parent, or child.

The Good Guy is a Hero • You and Joe walk out of class and into the parking lot. You see a guy approach a girl and pull out a gun. You run up from behind and hit him in the head with a metal stake, he falls and suffers a massive head wound. The school newspaper headline reads "STUDENT FOILS ROBBER," you become a local campus hero, and the girl you saved ultimately marries you after graduation. Although a bit risky, your quick action is heroic and legally justified under the circumstances.

The Good Guy is a Chump • You and Joe walk out of the bar one night and you see a man and a woman struggling next to a car. They are both yelling and she repeatedly says no, but the man grabs the keys, pushes her to the ground, and jumps in and begins to start the car. Joe quickly runs over and grabs him out of the car as it begins to drive off. As he falls from the car, his foot is crushed under the back wheel and the car runs into another car in the parking lot. As the cops arrive and begin to talk to everyone, it is apparent that the guy was just trying to keep her from driving his car home drunk and their argument had gotten out of control and he was trying to go home. Although Joe's quick action is admirable and you both honestly thought you were trying to save her property, Joe will probably escape prosecution, but no guarantee to that. Although you can't always know what is going on, try before you take drastic action. But sometimes you have to rely on your instincts and act.

What is a Reasonable Belief? • It is not necessary that there should be actual danger, as a person has the right to defend his life and person from apparent danger as fully and to the same extent as he would have were the danger real, as it reasonably appeared to him from his standpoint at the time. Remember, the use of deadly force against another is okay when and to the degree you reasonably believe the force is immediately necessary. Also remember, that a jury will decide what is reasonably necessary and to what degree.

What if Someone Else Gets Hurt? • Even though a person is justified in threatening or using force or deadly force against another, if in doing so he also recklessly injures or kills an innocent third person, the justifications or defense for that person's actions are unavailable in a prosecution for the reckless injury or killing of the innocent third person. If you are trying to prevent someone from committing suicide or from hurting themselves to the point they would have serious bodily injury, then you can use force to the degree he reasonably believes the force is immediately necessary, but not deadly force. If you're trying to save someone's life in an emergency then you can even use deadly force, to the degree you reasonably believe is immediately necessary to preserve the life.

GUNS
"Every citizen shall have the right to keep and bear arms in the lawful defense of himself or the State; but the Legislature shall have power, by law, to regulate the wearing of arms, with a view to prevent crime." Ownership of guns in Texas is about as Wild West as it gets in the U.S. Ownership of a Handgun, Shotgun, Rifle, and Semi-automatic assault weapons are unrestricted and no state permit or license is required, however ownership of a machine gun has federal law compliance issues, which must be strictly adhered to.

Shotguns & Rifles
Bubba's truck with the rifle or shotgun sitting right there in the gun rack of his pick-up, even if loaded, well hell, that's okay in Texas. We do not prohib-

it the transport of loaded rifles and shotguns in vehicles, whether in the rack or right on the seat next to you. Bubba can pack this type of heat, but can't have a handgun sitting on the seat, even unloaded. Go figure.

Handguns

Where it gets tricky is when and how you carry handguns. Carrying handguns "on or about one's person" on foot or in a vehicle is explicitly prohibited by statute. "On or about one's person" includes any handgun within arm's reach, either concealed or in the open, as well as under the seat, on the dash, in the glove compartment or even in the backseat. There is a specific exemption that allows you to carry handguns for self-protection while traveling across Texas on a "bonafide" journey or engaged in a lawfully related firearm activity such as hunting or target shooting.

Guns & Cars

While packing your car for the drive back to school after Thanksgiving, you luckily remembered to throw your shotgun in the back seat for the quail hunt next weekend and you grab Dad's old pistol and throw it in there also for some target practice while out in the fields. On the way back to school, you stop by to stay the night with your grandmother. Later that evening, Grandma sends you out for some milk, but while on the way back from the store, you roll through the only stop sign in town and the local Sheriff decides to stop you and see what's going on, especially because you're "not from 'round here are ya boy?" During the traffic stop, he sees the pistol sitting in the back seat and BANG you now find yourself calling Grammy from the slammer to bail you out.

Since you are technically traveling, the Sheriff probably should not arrest you for this questionable infraction, however any misunderstanding or doubt as to your traveler status, your intentions, or attitude (See Chapter 2), may all ultimately result in an overnight stay at the Crossbar Motel. If there is any question of your classification as bonafide traveler, such as an overnight stay or other break or side-trip from the journey, you really should carry the handgun unloaded and cased in the trunk, just in case.

If you are traveling to another state and you are spending at least one night away from home, you must carry the firearm and the ammunition secured in separate places and both outside of your reach. Under Federal law, you should be okay, but Federal law is pretty vague about what constitutes traveling, so be sure you will be staying over at least one night and have checked the states' laws.

Not only can handguns cause you a problem if you don't carry them properly, if you sell, rent, lease, loan, or give a handgun to anyone that you know intends to use it unlawfully or sell a handgun to someone who is intoxicated, other legal problems may arise from such activity.

Concealed Handgun License

A Texas Concealed Handgun License (CHL) allows a person to carry a handgun on one's person and in one's vehicle, but Texas law says you must keep your firearm concealed and you can carry as many as you can conceal. If you are interested in lawfully carrying a handgun, contact Texas DPS or a local certified instructor for class information and certification. The classes and certification are not difficult, but your attendance, attention, and shooting proficiency will be required. Your criminal background will also affect your ability to obtain a CHL. The basic requirements are:

1. Twenty-one years old when DPS receives your application;
2. resident of Texas for at least six months;

But, you will not be eligible if:

1. you've been convicted of a felony or Class A or B misdemeanor within the last five years;
2. you've been convicted of Class C misdemeanor Disorderly Conduct in the last five years;
3. you've been found by a court to be in default on any student loan, any state or city taxes, or in default on child support;
4. you're presently charged with a Felony, Class A or B Misdemeanor, or Class C Disorderly Conduct;
5. you are currently under a court protective order or subject to a restraining order affecting the spousal relationship, other than a restraining order solely affecting property interest;
6. have been adjudicated in the last ten years as having engaged in delinquent conduct violating a penal law of the grade of felony;
7. you made any material misrepresentation, or failed to disclose any material fact, in an application submitted to DPS;
8. you've been convicted twice within the last ten years for any Class B misdemeanor, or greater, involving the use of alcohol or a controlled substance; or,
9. you're a fugitive from justice; a chemically dependent person; or a person of unsound mind.

The Student Body of Law

The privilege to carry a concealed handgun granted by this license may or may not be valid in other states, so check with the Texas Department of Public Safety regarding reciprocity agreements with other states and those states' laws regarding your carrying in that state, even if just driving through.

Whether a citizen has a license to carry a handgun or not does not affect the right to use any firearm or other deadly weapon in defensive situations. This is completely dependant on the justification(s) to do so under the laws relating to self-defense as explained earlier.

Places Where You Cannot Carry Your Firearm (Licensed or Not):

Any property that has posted what is called a "30.06" sign. This is a sign that is about three feet wide, at least two feet high, and very conspicuous. The requirements are very precise and usually are not legally valid, but again don't test these limits. If you see one that basically complies, don't carry. Examples are:

1. Federal property, most of which will be marked with a sign that refers to Title 18 of the U.S. Code, usually the Post Office;
2. A school, or premises where a school activity is being conducted;
3. A polling place while voting is going on, either early voting or the day of the election. Be careful of this one with the early voting practices today, this could be almost anywhere or anytime. Look for the sign that says "No electioneering beyond this point" which marks the line past which you cannot carry your firearm;
4. Any government court or offices utilized by a court;
5. The premises of a racetrack;
6. The secured area of an airport (meaning past the metal detectors). With tightened security of post 9/11, you can probably carry into the non-secure areas, but again, this one can be dangerous with vehicle checks and that sort of thing;
7. Within 1,000 feet of a place of legal execution, (yes, execution of a prisoner);
8. A facility that derives 51% or more of its profits from the sale of alcoholic beverages for consumption on premise. Basically, night clubs, bars, and ice houses, but restaurants that serve alcohol and liquor stores are usually okay. If you can't, there will be a sign near the entrance with a red "51" on it. The "51" must be five inches high, so it will be conspicuous;
9. Premises where a high school, collegiate, or professional sport

ing event or interscholastic event is taking place, unless the license holder is a participant in the event and a handgun is used in the event;
10. Premises of a correctional facility;
11. Premises of a hospital or nursing home (if posted with a 30.06 sign), due to the oxygen systems in the walls;
12. An amusement park (if posted with a 30.06 sign);
13. Premises of a church, synagogue, or other established place of religious worship (if posted with a 30.06 sign);
14. A meeting of a governmental entity (if posted with a 30.06 sign), usually City Council meetings, etc.;
15. Your employer can forbid you to carry without posting a 30.06 sign if it is mentioned in your employee handbook or on any form you are required to sign; and,
16. Private property where the owner or person in effective control asks you to leave, in which case you have to leave immediately. For this to happen in the real world, the person in control of the property would first have to see the licensee's firearm, which would place them in violation anyway, and then confront an armed individual to ask them to leave.

The long and the short of it is that if you want to carry a handgun, get a license to do so. Know the law and do so responsibly. If you hunt, shoot trap and/or sporting clays or just target shoot, know the rules and transport your weapons unloaded and in the right place. The quickest way to get an already nervous police officer more nervous is to either produce a gun or have one where it's not supposed to be.

OTHER WEAPONS

Handguns and rifles are not the only weapons that you cannot carry around. The "carrying" aspect of this is the same as discussed above, but also includes possessing, manufacturing, transporting, repairing, or selling a(n): handgun; illegal knife; club; explosive weapon; machine gun; short-barrel firearm; firearm silencer; switchblade knife; knuckles ("brass knuckles"); armor-piercing ammunition; chemical dispensing device; or zip gun.

Law enforcement officers and military personnel are exempted, as are switchblade knives, springblade knives, and short-barrel firearms, but only if they are antiques or curios.

CHAPTER EIGHT
Apartments, Leases, Housing

FINDING YOUR NEW PAD

You have served your time in the dorms and you are now able to look for off-campus housing; maybe an apartment by yourself or an old house with five others to share rent and expenses. Maybe your dorm has been overrun with rats or your roommate has dropped out of school and you have two weeks to find a new place to live. Your options are your car, a friend's couch for the rest of the semester, or a quick decision to sign a lease.

Before you sign, take your time and make sure you've read and understand all of the language in the lease, including the fine print.

In any event, after an extensive search through the classified section of the newspaper or driving around looking for the "for lease" signs, you find the right place. Someone else is looking also and the person showing you the property tells you, it will go fast. You're anxious to sign the lease as soon as it is placed in front of you. Hold on a second; resist the urge. What makes you think that your best interests as a tenant will be protected? You are responsible for your own decisions now, so look out for yourself. Your desire to find a place after long hours searching can push you into signing on the dotted line. Before you sign, take your time and make sure you've read and understand all of the language in the lease, including the fine print.

THE LEASE

A couple of terms you should know:
1. Lessee – The tenant (person renting the property);
2. Lessor – The Landlord (person who owns or manages the property);
3. Lease – the actual written document that is the lease contract.

There are many more purposes for a lease, other than your agreement to pay your rent each month and maintain your apartment in good condition. Most important are the responsibilities of your landlord, which should be clearly outlined in this contract, so it's obviously in your best interests to read the lease carefully. If you're ignorant of the lease terms, you could find yourself blindsided several months later when your landlord holds you responsible for damage or some other breach of the lease and subsequently asks you to move out. What if you've got to move before your lease expires? The lease will outline your financial obligations should you need to back out for any reason.

Some leasing offices and landlords will place a lengthy, "standard" lease in front of you and downplay or simplify its terms. They're probably not trying to trick you, but are really more likely in a hurry. Don't let their schedule dictate your decision and don't ever feel pressured or hurried; instead, move off to the side, allow the leasing agent/landlord to accommodate other potential tenants and take your time to continue reading the lease until you understand all of its terms. Make sure to take time to look for the sections dealing with late payment of rent penalties, maintenance responsibilities, and any prohibited activity. Even if you've read and signed a lease before, don't think they're all the same; they're not. Once you sign the lease and give a deposit, you're usually locked into its terms for at least will forfeit the deposit if you don't move in. Find out before signing what the consequences will be if you change your mind before moving day: like will you get your full deposit back?

You may not realize that under the law, you're entitled to request changes to the lease before signing it. In fact, you can request any modification you want, so don't be afraid or intimidated from asking for changes. Remember, the person you are dealing with may be the same person you have to deal with when you want something fixed or the return of the deposit, so be reasonable and respectful during the initial negotiations. If the landlord agrees to your terms, make sure the new terms are written on the lease itself (in ink, not pencil), dated with both party's initials next to them. Make sure you are given a copy of the executed lease before you leave and always keep a copy. Verbal promises will never hold up in the event that you have a disagreement over lease terms with your landlord in the future.

Let's say you've agreed to lease the property, but only if they replace the carpet, fix the leaking toilet, and allow your Labrador Retriever to live with you; get it in writing with the date and a signature. If the landlord refuses to put any of the verbal agreement(s) in writing or suddenly makes some excuse why it shouldn't be included, warning bells should go off. No matter how cool the pad is, a bad landlord can make any place a miserable place to live. Move on and keep looking for the right place.

What if it's too late? You signed the lease and moved in without getting the new verbal agreements in writing and now you keep requesting that those agreements be satisfied, like maintenance or repairs that have never been done. Threatening to withhold payment of your rent isn't a good idea. If there were a court battle, there's a good chance your landlord will win if you withhold rent payments without a signed agreement detailing your right to do so. Not only could you be facing stiff monetary penalties, you could find yourself evicted and out on the street looking for another place to live. The State Bar of Texas suggests that tenants who withhold rent and use their deposits instead, when their leases did not state they could do so, can face monetary penalties of up to three times the amount of rent they withheld.

There are really only three situations where a tenant can withhold rent:

1. If the tenant first received a court order allowing him/her to withhold rent, if the landlord didn't perform agreed-upon repairs or meet various conditions;
2. If the tenant made repairs in his or her own unit and paid for them out of pocket; if the landlord was aware of and approved those repairs and the lease clearly stated that deductions in rent could be made under those circumstances; or,
3. If you have legally terminated your lease because your landlord or apartment management company broke the terms of your written lease agreement with respect to his or her responsibility for repairs, or if your utilities have been cut off unlawfully.

Usually, those who have rental property, especially in college towns, are not there to take advantage of the students. The rental property market is probably good and they have and probably will continue to make a handsome profit from their investment property, but they are also interested in preserving their property in good order to continue to keep the property profitable.

The bottom line is that you should always look out for yourself when entering into any kind of contract or lease.

MOVING IN

Now you've done your homework, found the right place, read the fine print, understand all the terms, signed the lease, and paid the deposit. One last thing before you move in. Inspect the property thoroughly. Make notes of all defects, no matter how small. If there is rust in the sink, write it down, small nail holes in the wall, write it down. If the door doesn't shut properly, write it down, toilet flushes funny, make a note. Take pictures of these conditions if possible and make the landlord sign off and date all of your notations, and give him/her a copy and you keep the original. This will come in handy down the road when you move out and any dispute arises over the return of your deposit.

REPAIRS

Now you've actually moved in and started living in your new home, hopefully attending class and studying on occasion. Ideally, your landlord is easily accessible for repairs or other issues and takes care of their business. However, if they don't and you need a repair, make your requests in writing, sent through the US mail with a return receipt requested (it costs a little more than just the stamp), but anytime you want to make sure someone got a letter or notice, this is a green card that is signed by the person it is sent to. The green card is then sent to the sender (you) and the stamped green card is admissible in court to prove that someone got the letter. Documentation is essential, keep your lease and any paperwork or receipts relating to the property. Don't rely on a phone call, it doesn't prove a thing. Put it in writing. Some minor repairs are your responsibility and if your rent payments are current, the landlord or management must make repairs within a reasonable time to correct conditions that threaten your health or safety. This can be anything from plumbing and electrical problems to common areas of the property in some instances. Look over your lease to see if it details your responsibilities for repairs. If not, then it falls upon the landlord to keep the property in proper repair and condition as it was when the lease was signed and you moved in.

The last resort is to make repairs yourself. This is only after you have made the requests, put the landlord on notice, and no repairs are made within a reasonable time. You may make the repairs yourself and deduct that amount from the next month's rent. This, however, is a last resort and one that may have some risks involved. Double-check your lease and be sure that you have given the landlord all opportunity to make the repairs before resorting to making the repairs yourself.

The landlord or management cannot retaliate against tenants who ask for repairs. An eviction, rent increase or other adverse action within six months of a request for repairs is presumed to be retaliatory unless the landlord can show a valid reason for their actions.

THE MONTH TO MONTH LEASE

Let's say you've lived in the house or apartment and your lease date is almost up. The lease does not automatically expire and you have to move out. If nothing happens and you pay the rent and the check is cashed, then the lease automatically becomes a month to month lease. This means that so long as you pay the rent on time and the landlord cashes the checks without giving some form of notice, this arrangement continues until one of the parties makes a change.

LEASE TERMINATION – SPLITTING OR THROWN OUT?

Your lease is almost up and either you want to move or the landlord wants you out. The party that wants to terminate the lease must give notice before the rent due date or lease termination date, usually the same. The amount of notice required is usually in the lease and it is usually thirty days. That means that the party that wants to terminate the lease must give the other party at least thirty days written notice. If they don't give at least thirty days notice, then the notice rolls over to the next rent due date. For example, lets say that the lease is set to end on January 31st and the rent is due on the first day of the month. You got notice on January 3rd from the landlord that he/she is terminating the lease and is requesting you vacate the property by February 1st. You actually have until March 1st, because you are entitled to at least thirty days notice in our example or however many days the lease dictates, but no less than what it dictates. Basically, if either party does not give at least the amount of notice necessary, it rolls over into a month to month lease, at least for that one month, but so long as the rent is paid on time, the rent check is cashed by the landlord and no notice is given, then the other terms of the lease remains intact and the lease remains enforceable by either party.

LOCK OUT & EVICTION -

One afternoon, you are be-bopping back to the pad for your usual afternoon nap. You get to the door and your key doesn't work. You realize that the landlord has locked you out and, more importantly, locked your stuff inside. You think back to the last time you paid rent and all those late notices the landlord kept sending you. Generally speaking, the landlord does not have the right to lock you out for failing to pay the rent. Before locking you out, your landlord must tell you when the locks will be changed and where you can get new keys, without having to pay any of the owed rent.

The landlord must go through eviction proceedings to forcibly remove someone from there home. All evictions require an order signed by a judge and usually takes several months to go through the procedures to evict someone. If you find yourself in this situation or are served with legal papers, usually a suit for forcible entry and detainer, immediately contact an attorney or seek legal advice through your school. Usually student services has an attorney available for counsel.

SECURITY DEPOSIT

The end of the semester is coming up and you plan to backpack through Europe for the first half of the summer and follow Widespread Panic for the other half. You are going to put your Futon, milk crates and cinder blocks in storage for the summer. You have given the proper amount of notice that you are terminating the lease and moving out, usually at least thirty days prior to move out. Remember that security deposit you put up before moving in and are planning to have in hand for your travels? Good news, you are entitled to get that back, so long as the property has not suffered from you living there. You have some responsibilities to comply with if you want to get some or all of your deposit money back. Vacating the property clean and without any unusual damage, only normal wear and tear, will usually do the trick, but taking the time and making the effort to make small repairs, such as nail holes in the walls or any other small repairs will help. Lastly, remove everything, including all trash, and clean the whole apartment This is a common area that landlords like to use to keep a portion, if not all of the deposit.

Just like when you moved-in, when you are ready to turn over the keys, get your list of defects that you made when you moved-in and go through the property with the landlord to compare; take ample pictures of the condition of the property when you left it.

The Student Body of Law

Landlords are not entitled to keep your deposit without a valid reason. The lease should give you a good idea of what is expected of you upon vacating the property. If you have been out for over thirty days, write the landlord a letter, send it return receipt requested, making demand of the deposit or an itemized accounting and reasons for its retention. When you get the landlord's response, compare their complaints with your list of defects you made when you moved in. Remember when you did that? Now find it wherever you put it. This will help if you have to fight the landlord for the return of the deposit. If he/she has good reason for using the deposit to make repairs, such as the hole in the carpet from your dog's incessant digging and chewing, or the huge red punch stain left from that birthday party you had for three hundred of your closest friends, then you may consider writing it off. But if you have taken care of the place, cleaned it before you left, and didn't destroy the place, you should get most, if not all of your deposit back.

Remember, you are not entitled to skip that last month's rent payment, thinking the security deposit will cover it, unless the lease specifically states that this is an option.

The real key to enjoying where you live is your relationship with the landlord or manager. Keep it friendly but business-like and you will have a much better chance at getting the repairs you need taken care of, avoiding any unpleasant confrontations. Eventually, you'll get your deposit back in full.

MOVING? DON'T FORGET TO FORWARD YOUR ADDRESS

Since you are probably a student, you are going to move a lot. Probably every year, sometimes more. Even after school, you'll move for new jobs, back home, and away again. Wherever your mailing address is, if you ever move, remember to go to the US Post Office and fill-out the change of address form so your mail will be forwarded to you new address. Change your address on your driver's license and bills. The most important reasons for doing this is just in case you got a ticket, forgot about it, and it's gone to warrant or a bill hasn't been paid. If these go into the "undeliverable" bin, then you'll never know about it and it will eventually come back to haunt you, wreck your credit, or maybe even get you a night in jail when you least expect it.

LIVING WITH ROOMMATES

You have found the best place to live, but you need one or a couple of roommate(s) to help out with the rent and bills. No problem, your best friend needs a place too, and what fun you'll have sharing a place. Conflicts can arise between even old friends who now are living together. Like that annoying habit your roommate has of leaving the dishes in the sink for over a month or the stereo playing at full force at 4 a.m. the night before your mid-terms. There is no magical advice that will help with personality conflicts, just some helpful advice from someone who has been there:

1) Know who it is that you are planning on living with, their particular habits and living needs, if possible, even their girlfriend or boyfriend. You may find that you spend almost as much time with them as the roommate;
2) Be tolerant of those annoying habits and needs, if possible;
3) Be considerate of your roommate, remembering that your habits may also be annoying to them;
4) Talk about and address problems as they arise, without letting them multiply, ultimately resulting in a confrontation and heated argument;
5) Try to remember that you were friends before living together, so you must be able to get along, try to do so now as roommates, go out have a beer and talk it out as friends;
6) Establish some basic responsibilities that each has for the common good of the house (bills, cleaning, etc.), but remember don't go overboard with the rules, and,
7) Be flexible

If you sign a lease and your roommate doesn't, then you will be held responsible for whatever damage they may ultimately cause and will be solely responsible for the rent. Most leases will require all persons residing to be on the lease. However, this is not always a disadvantage. If you are the only person on the lease, then you can control who lives there, but make sure to check the lease provisions regarding the number of persons allowed to reside on the premises. If you chose to do this, remember, you have now technically become a sub-lessor and are sub-

The Student Body of Law

ject to the same constraints as the lessor or landlord to your tenants.

THE AMENITIES OF MODERN LIFE
(ELECTRIC, PHONE, CABLE TV AND UTILITIES)

Now that you have a place, you'll need electricity, water and/or gas service, telephone, and maybe even cable/satellite TV. All of these are services that can be applied for and sometimes require a deposit before an account can be opened with the local power, telephone, and various other utility companies in your area. Many times, a person who already has an active account can co-sign for your new account, thus relieving the need for a deposit. The only drawback is that the co-signer is agreeing to be held responsible for payment if you don't take care of the account when due.

Setting up these accounts does not usually present a problem that can't be overcome, however it is important to take these accounts seriously. For most students, these are the first credit-based accounts and can be the first steps in establishing positive credit ratings. The real problem is if they are reported as default accounts that go uncollected, it can trigger collection agencies that will hound you for years and create negative credit ratings, affecting your ability to buy a car or house. Most people, especially students, don't realize these possibilities until it is too late. Take the responsibility to pay these accounts as they come due and this basic cornerstone of establishing a positive credit report will be well worth the effort later in life.

TRESPASSING

A person commits the offense of trespassing if he/she enters or remains on the property without the effective consent or remains in a building of another without the effective consent and that person had notice that his/her entry was forbidden or received notice to depart, but failed to do so.

Notice can mean one of several different things:
1) Oral or written communication by the owner or someone with apparent authority to act for the owner;
2) Fencing or other enclosure obviously designed to exclude intruders or to contain livestock;
3) A sign or signs posted on the property or at the entrance to the building reasonable likely to come to the attention of the intruders, indicating entry is forbidden;
4) The placement of identifying purple paint marks on trees or posts

on the property, provided that the marks are:
- (i) vertical lines of not less than eight inches in length and not less than one inch in width;
- (ii) placed so that the bottom of the mark is not less than three feet from the ground or more than five feet from the ground;
- (iii) placed at locations that are readily visible to any person approaching the property and no more than:
   - (a) 100 feet apart on forest land;
   - (b) 1,000 feet apart on land other than forest land;
   or
5) The visible presence on the property of a crop grown for human consumption that is under cultivation, in the process of being harvested, or marketable if harvested at the time of entry.

Trespassing is generally a Class B Misdemeanor- a Class C Misdemeanor if it is on agricultural land- but is always a Class A Misdemeanor if the actor carries a deadly weapon (i.e. firearm) about his person during the commission of the trespass.

The most important thing to remember from this section is that if someone is on your property or in your house that you do not want there, simply inform them that they are no longer welcome and ask that they leave. If they refuse and stay, or leave and enter again, this will allow you to call the police to have them arrested for trespassing. You must allow them a reasonable opportunity to leave before the police will do anything, but it may become necessary to either prevent someone from entering your property or ejecting someone who has worn out their welcome. Not to mention if you are asked to leave someone's house or property, including a place of business and/or club/bar/party and you remain, you could be subject to arrest for trespassing. This exclusion can even extend into the future without end.

For example, you and Joe are at the local icehouse having some pops with your pals. After some hours of merriment, your group decides it would be great fun to hold a fencing tournament on top of several pool tables, implementing the pool cues as foils for the matches. The manager approaches and informs you that you all are no longer welcome and asked not only to leave, but also never come back. If one or more of you refuse to leave at this time, the manager is well within his rights to either forcibly remove you from the

The Student Body of Law

premises or call the cops to arrest you for trespassing. Months later, you forget about the ugly display of drunkenness, not to mention the terribly bad form displayed during your fencing match and return with your girlfriend to the icehouse for a relaxing adult beverage. The manager recognizes you and again, is well within his right to either forcibly remove you or call the cops to arrest you.

By the way, fire fighters and emergency services personnel are excluded from the trespass statute, so long as they are acting in the lawful discharge of an official duty under exigent circumstances.

PARKING

Certainly, you can see the situation where a landlord may want to tow your car out of the apartment parking lot. Granted, it leaks oil as fast as you can fill it and the tires always lose their air in three days, but before it can be towed away, there are some pretty specific rules that apply to this type of situation. First, apartment complex parking is defined as a parking facility serving or adjacent to an apartment complex consisting of one or more residential apartment units and any adjacent real property serving the apartment complex.

There are some basic rules that any owner cannot break, but there are some that *you* cannot as well. You may not leave unattended on a parking facility a vehicle that: obstructs a gate that is designed or intended for the use of pedestrians or vehicles; or obstructs pedestrian or vehicular access to a common garbage collection area that is used for the placement of garbage; or obstructs restricted parking space(s); or is in a properly marked tow away zone (brightly painted and is conspicuously and legibly marked with the warning "TOW AWAY ZONE" in contrasting letters at least three inches tall); or is a semi-truck, unless specifically permitted under the terms of the lease; or is leaking a fluid that presents a hazard or threat to persons or property. This last one is the killer for most poor college students.

The following are commonly used by property management, but are not valid. The landlord CANNOT tow your car merely because the vehicle does not display: an un-expired license plate or registration insignia, or a valid vehicle inspection sticker for this or another state or country. A contract provision providing for the removal for these reasons is valid only if the provision requires the owner or operator of the vehicle to be given at least ten days' written notice that the vehicle will be towed from the facility at the vehicle owner's or operator's expense if it is not removed from the parking facility.

The notice must be: 1) delivered in person to the owner or operator of the vehicle; or 2) sent by certified mail, return receipt requested, to that owner or operator. Any provision of an apartment lease that is in conflict or inconsistent with this section is void and may not be enforced.

CHAPTER NINE
Transportation

BUYING AND SELLING CARS, MOTORCYCLES, JET SKIS, ETC.

This section is entitled "Transportation" and will examine all forms of motorized travel. As you may have seen around campus, various modes of transportation are used, but the car is still king and one of the more complex, common, and responsibility-laden pieces of property we own. The two most complex events regarding our cars, other than understanding the complex internal workings and various systems that make the car, well, a car, is the purchase and sale of the car. We will address the fundamentals of these transactions so you will be able to understand them and safely and successfully buy or sell a car. A car, motorcycle, jet ski, and boat are all basically just like any other property and can be sold by anyone who owns it. This is the first hurdle.

Tip!

The lien is the legal mechanism or instrument/document that lets the lien-holder let everyone know that they have a right to some money if the property is sold.

LIENS

If you own a car and are making payments on it, you don't actually own the car outright. The bank or finance company actually has the title because they fronted you the money to buy the car. They are the first lien-holder on the car. A lien-holder is someone who is owed money for the property and must be paid first, if the property is sold. The lien is the legal mechanism or instrument/document that lets the lien-holder let everyone know that they have a right to some money if the property is sold. For instance, if you sold your car and still owed the bank some of the money they loaned you to buy the car, they would get paid before releasing the title to the new buyer. They retain a partial ownership interest in the car to protect them if they don't get paid. So if you are selling a car and still owe money on it, be mindful that before the person gets the title, you will have to pay off the balance owed to the bank. When you pay off the balance owed to the bank, they normally send you the title to do with it as you please. It is this situation that most people find themselves in when selling a car.

TITLES

If you have the title, you will see that it is labeled "Texas Certificate of Title" and will have all identifying information regarding the vehicle. It will also list the previous owner, the current owner, and any lien-holders. The title should be signed by the current owner. If the title is clear of liens, either the lien-holder section will be blank or there will be some writing next to the lien-holder section that indicates that the lien has been released.

On the back of the title are the pertinent parts that will allow either sale or transfer of the title. The top portion deals with a situation where one person wants to sell the vehicle to another person or transfer title to another person without necessarily selling it to them. All requested information should be printed on the title indicating the name and address of the buyer, the odometer reading, the signature of the seller, the printed name of the seller, the signature of the buyer, and the printed name of the buyer. Once the sale is complete, the seller gives the buyer the title.

SALES AGREEMENT

It is always a good idea to write out a short and concise sales agreement or bill of sale that spells out the transaction. All this document needs to say is that the seller agrees to sell the car to the buyer, including the sale price, the date of the sale/transfer, and any other particular terms of the sale. For instance, you may want to state that the sale is "as is" or that the seller does not guarantee or give a warranty that the car will operate or perform in any way. You may also put a provision in the document that states that the buyer agrees that the car has been inspected by them and it is in the condition and working order that they expect when they purchased the car. Don't worry about the language, as long as it says simply what is being sold, for what price and any conditions of the sale that may apply or that you want clear in case there is a misunderstanding later, it's fine.

Another document that will be required for transfer is the odometer affidavit. This document must be completed by the seller: who verifies the

The Student Body of Law

odometer reading and whether or not the seller believes the reading to be correct. It does not affect the sale either way, but is recorded and kept on file for future sales/transfers in tracking the odometer readings of that particular vehicle. It is the responsibility of the buyer to take the title and several other documents (identification & insurance) to the local county clerk's office to have registration and title transferred into the buyer's name. There will be fees involved and you will also have to pay sales tax on the sale of the car. Be prepared to pay approximately eight percent of the selling price, depending on the county or municipality of the sale.

OWNING & DRIVING INSURANCE

If you're going to drive, you need insurance for several different and good reasons. First, it's the law in Texas that if you operate a motor vehicle, you must be able to demonstrate financial responsibility for damages to other cars or property and injuries you may cause. Secondly, losses from property damage,

medical and legal costs, and lost income add up to billions of dollars annually for automobile mishaps. Automobile insurance can protect you from serious financial losses that can result from an accident.

If you can, use an insurance agent that your family has used over the years. If not, call around to some of the local insurance agencies and if you find one you like, use them. It's always a good idea to have someone close you can stop by or call if you have specific questions or problems. That's why insurance agents are there.

The basic types of auto insurance coverage include:

Bodily Injury Liability: Pays your legal defense costs and claims against you if your car injures or kills someone. Covers family members living with you and others driving with your permission.

Property Damage Liability: Pays your legal defense costs and claims against you if your car damages another's property. Does not cover your property, including your auto.

Medical Payments or Personal Injury Protection: Pays medical expenses resulting from an accident for you and others riding in your car. Also pays for you or your family members injured while riding in another's car or while walking.

Collision: Pays for repairs of damage to your car caused by a collision with another vehicle or any other object, regardless of who was responsible.

Comprehensive Physical Damage: Pays for damages to your car resulting from theft, fire, hail, vandalism, or a variety of other causes.

Uninsured or Underinsured Motorist: Pays for costs related to injuries or property damage to you or your family members and guests in your car caused by an uninsured, underinsured, or hit-and-run driver.

HOW CAN I LOWER MY CAR INSURANCE?

Young, male drivers are considered by the insurance companies to be the highest risk to insure, so you may want to try and save a few bucks on your insurance costs. Call around and get several quotes. The process of determining your insurance rate is determinative of your rating. There are lots of factors that go into someone's rating, so there are some things you can do to reduce the costs, like asking for higher deductibles. Deductibles are the amounts of money you pay before your insurance company kicks in. By raising the deductibles on collision and comprehensive (fire and theft) coverage, you can lower your insurance costs substantially, sometimes by fifteen to thirty percent.

You can also drop the Comprehensive/Collision Coverages if your car is an old car. If your car is worth less than $2,000, it may not be cost-effective to keep this coverage, but the risk is that if you are in an accident the costs to fix your car is on you. If you don't know the value of your car, go to the Kelly Blue Book available at a library or at www.kbb.com. You can also buy a "Low Profile, Low Maintenance" car. Cars that are expensive to repair or that are the popular targets of car thieves have higher insurance costs. See the National Insurance Crime Bureau at web site www.nicb.org for a list of the U.S.' top stolen vehicles. Some companies offer discounts to motorists who drive fewer than a predetermined number of miles a year, so ask when getting a quote. Premium costs tend to be lowest in rural communities and highest in cities, so if you are going to school in a small town or outside the major metropolitan areas, register the car there. If your car has automatic seat belts, airbags and anti-lock brakes you might get a discount. Some insurers offer

The Student Body of Law

discounts for a variety of other qualifications like: no accidents in three years; driver training courses; other anti-theft devices; good grades; and having more than one car insured with that company, so going through your parents' company may be beneficial.

Words you may need to know before purchasing auto insurance:

Conditions: Explanations in the policy of your responsibilities and the company's, such as how claims are to be filed and what documentation should be submitted with a claim.

Coverage: Description in the policy of the specific circumstances under which you receive benefits.

Declarations: Listing of the details of your particular coverage, such as the policy number, kinds of coverage and amounts of money provided by each, your name and address, a description of your vehicle, the premium, and coverage duration.

Exclusions: Descriptions of the situations under which you and your car are not covered.

Premium: The cost of the insurance policy (usually paid out in monthly, quarterly, by-annual or annual payments).

WHAT THE HECK IS SR-22?

An SR-22 is DPS Form SR-22 and it is the form that insurance companies file with the DPS to verify and certify that you have insurance. The insurance company must notify DPS anytime the policy is cancelled, terminated or lapses. SR-22 insurance is not necessarily high-risk insurance, but the insurance company will be quite curious as to why it is that you need it. You don't even have to own a car to get an SR-22.

PARKING & THE TOW TRUCK

As is your usual custom, you pull into an open spot close to campus. You notice the parking meter, but as is your custom, do not put any money in. After class, yet again, parking ticket is on the window. You stuff it into the glove box. One day after class, you return to your parking space, but your car is gone. It's unlikely that your prized 1976 Buick Electra has been lifted. You've been towed. You recall a similar situation last semester when you told your buddy, Joe to just park close to the club and not to worry about the NO

PARKING sign. Again, to your surprise, the car was not there after a night of revelry. In these cases, you have been lawfully towed. Some cities have instituted what is known as The Boot. This is a large steel cuff (usually painted bright yellow or red) that attaches to the cars wheel and immobilizes it until you contact the city and pay up.

Police officers have the authority to tow a vehicle whose driver has been arrested, that has been in a collision and cannot be driven safely, or any other situation in which they reasonably feel necessary to remove the vehicle to clear traffic obstructions, or if the vehicle is an instrument or evidence of a crime. Your car may be towed for numerous reasons from a private parking lot, such as obstructing a portion of a paved drive or abutting public road; obstructs a traffic aisle, entry, or exit of the parking facility; prevents a vehicle from exiting a parking space in the facility; obstructs a marked fire lane; does not display the special license plates or placard for disabled parking or other unauthorized space.

PRIVATE PARKING LOTS

Before you can be towed, you must have notice that parking there may result in towing or is otherwise prohibited. Signs prohibiting unauthorized vehicles must be present at the time of towing and for the preceding 24-hours. Other proper notice is: a conspicuous notice attached to the vehicle's front windshield that states: why it is improperly parked; where proper parking is authorized; notice that towing may occur if it remains; and, a 24-hour telephone number that will locate the towed vehicle.

NO PARKING SIGNS

In order for a NO PARKING sign to be adequate, it must be: facing and conspicuously visible to the driver of a vehicle that enters the facility, located on the side of each driveway and/or entrance or if no definite entrances exist, at twenty-five foot intervals, and must be permanently mounted on a pole, post, permanent wall, or permanent barrier so that the bottom edge of the sign is no lower than five feet and no higher than eight feet above ground level. The sign must also must be made of weather-resistant material, at least eighteen inches wide and twenty-four inches tall, with the international symbol for towing vehicles with a statement describing who may park in the parking facility and prohibiting all others; bearing the words "Unauthorized Vehicles Will Be Towed at Owner's or Operator's Expense"; the days and hours of

The Student Body of Law

towing enforcement; and a 24-hour telephone number that will locate the vehicle. There are some other specific color, symbol and letter height requirements in the Texas Transportation Code, but these are the major requirements.

APARTMENT PARKING

Refer to the end of Chapter 8 dealing with apartment living. There are some different rules that cover apartment complex parking, which is defined as a parking facility serving or adjacent to an apartment complex consisting of one or more residential apartment units and any adjacent real property serving the apartment complex.

SO YOUR CAR HAS BEEN WRONGFULLY TOWED

There were no signs posted, or the meter was broken, or your car was not abandoned, or leaking, or you feel the fees charged by the tow company and storage lot are way too high. You certainly have some rights when it comes to a towed vehicle and you have some action you can take.

If you think you were towed without probable cause, you can contest the tow through the court system at a special "tow hearing" created by Section 685 of the Texas Transportation Code. Tow hearings are held more quickly and have lower filing fees than many other types of hearings. They are heard by the Justice of the Peace in whose jurisdiction the location from which the vehicle was removed, or in a municipality with a population of 1.9 million or more, a hearing under this chapter is before a judge of a municipal court.

TOW HEARING

In order to request a "tow hearing", you must do so by delivering a written request for the hearing to the court before the fourteenth day after the date the vehicle was removed and placed in the vehicle storage facility, excluding Saturdays, Sundays, and legal holidays. Your request for a hearing must contain: 1) the name, address, and telephone number of the owner or operator of the vehicle: 2) the location from which the vehicle was removed; 3) the date when the vehicle was removed; 4) the name, address, and telephone number of the person or law enforcement agency that authorized the removal; 5) the name, address, and telephone number of the vehicle storage facility in which the vehicle was placed; 6) the name, address, and telephone number of the towing company that removed the vehicle; 7) a copy of any receipt or notification that the owner or operator received from the towing company or the vehicle storage facility; and 8) if the vehicle was removed from a parking facility include: A) one or more photographs that show the location and text of any sign posted at the facility restricting parking of vehicles; or B) a statement that no sign restricting parking was posted at the parking facility. There may be a ten dollar filing fee that you will have to pay the court when filing for the hearing.

If you pay the tow and storage fees and pick-up your car before there is a hearing or before you request a hearing, the towing company or vehicle storage facility that received the payment must give you written notice of your rights to a hearing. The fourteen-day limit starts when you picked-up your car. This notice should give you all the information you will need to draft the request for hearing, including where you should file it.

Okay. You've done everything that's required for your day in court. What happens now? The Court must hear your case within seven days from receiving your request for a hearing and will notify you and the person or law enforcement agency that authorized the removal of the vehicle of the date, time, and place of the hearing. The issues to be determined by the court in this type of hearing are: 1) whether probable cause existed for the removal and placement of the vehicle; 2) whether a towing charge imposed or collected in connection with the removal or placement of the vehicle was greater than the amount authorized by the political subdivision under Section 643.201 or 643.203; 3) whether a towing charge imposed or collected in connection with the removal or placement of the vehicle was greater than the amount authorized under Section 643.204 or 643.205; or 4) whether a towing charge imposed or collected in connection with the removal or placement of the vehicle was greater than the amount filed with the department under Section 643.207.

If you request a tow hearing, do your homework and be prepared with pictures or witnesses that can attest to and support your position in addressing the issues above.

After the hearing, the court will make written findings of fact and a conclusions of law and may award: 1) court costs to the prevailing party; 2) the reasonable cost of photographs submitted under Section 685.007(b)(8) to a vehicle owner or operator who is the prevailing party; and 3) an amount equal

The Student Body of Law

to the amount that the towing charge exceeded fees regulated by a political subdivision or authorized by this code or by Chapter 2303, Occupations Code.

If you request a tow hearing, do your homework and be prepared with pictures or witnesses that can attest to and support your position in addressing the issues above. Be respectful of the court and dress appropriately. These will help in obtaining a favorable ruling.

SO YOUR CAR HAS BEEN LAWFULLY TOWED

First off, find out where your car is. Scrape up the money, get a ride to the storage lot and get it out as soon as you can. It can get really expensive to leave your car in the storage lot. Every day it's there, it racks up another day's storage fee on top of the original towing fee and there are other fees that are tacked on, such as a ten dollar preservation fee, which is charged if a tow truck or yard operator rolls up the window in the rain, as well as a call fee levied if the lot calls the owner to let them know that their vehicle is at the lot. Usually, city ordinances regulate how much an owner has to pay to get their car back, but I promise, it will not suit your budget to leave it in there until you think you can afford to get it out.

DAMAGES FROM TOW OR STORAGE

Now when you go to pick up that cherry ride of yours, remember to check it out before you sign any release.

Now when you go to pick up that cherry ride of yours, remember to check it out before you sign any release. Be reasonable in your assessment of any damages and if there is damage from either the tow or occurring while in storage, you may consider making a note of it on any release required by the storage lot. Get a copy, with their signature on it, as well as request in writing their insurance provider and their policy number. You may consider filing a written claim with the tow truck company, storage facility, and/or their respective insurance company. If you can take some pictures of the damage while still at the storage lot, do that also.

A parking lot owner who causes the removal of an unauthorized vehicle is not liable for damages arising from the removal or storage of the vehicle if the vehicle was lawfully towed by a towing company insured against liability for property damage incurred in towing a vehicle, and stored by a vehicle storage facility insured against liability for property damage incurred in storing a vehicle.

A towing company or parking facility owner who unlawfully tows a vehicle is liable for damages arising from the tow or storage of the vehicle, as well as all fees for towing and storage related to the illegal tow. Proof of negligence of a parking facility owner or towing company who has unlawfully towed a vehicle is not required to recover these damages and a towing company or parking facility owner who illegally tows intentionally, knowingly, or recklessly is liable to the owner or operator of the vehicle for $300, plus three times the amount of fees assessed in the vehicle's removal, towing, or storage, as well as any attorney's fees incurred by the owner.

THE VALET

After a great dinner with your new girlfriend, the valet wheels up in your vintage Yugo, but you immediately notice that the side mirror is ripped off and a nice scrape runs down the length of the car. You ask what happened. The reply is "Nothing."

It is a violation of Texas law to operate a valet parking service unless they have insurance for each employee who operates a motor vehicle for the service. This must include liability, comprehensive, general liability, garage insurance policy, a surety bond, or a deposit in the amount of $450,000. Not only do they have to carry insurance, but they must also exhibit, for public inspection, evidence of financial responsibility at a public accommodation whose patrons use the service.

Back to your Yugo. Ask to see their insurance, get the policy number, the insurance carrier, the names of all witnesses present, the name of the owner and take a picture if you have a camera handy. Ask to talk to the owner, if present, and try to iron it out immediately. Handle it just like a traffic accident.

ROUTINE MAINTENANCE
INSPECTION & REGISTRATION

One of the quickest ways to call attention to yourself and almost beg a police officer to pull you over is to let the inspection sticker or registration expire

The Student Body of Law

on your car. These two things can totally legitimize an officer's stop, which we have seen in earlier chapters, and can develop into other problematic situations. Keep your car up-to-date and in proper working condition and street-legal. This simple maintenance may be the most valuable in this entire book and may help keep you from having other, larger legal problems.

REPAIRS & MECHANICS

Every car will need maintenance and repairs and it is important to keep all inspection and registration up-to-date, but equally important is to keep your car properly maintained. If you are so inclined, do the work yourself, but if you do not possess these talents you will have to depend on the local mechanic to keep that "jewel of the road" you own humming along. Try to use a shop that someone else recommends, if possible and take someone with you just to see and hear what is said and agreed upon. When you take the car in, make sure they take the time to listen to what you need fixed or explain exactly the problem you're having, even write it down for them on the work order. Do not sign anything until you first read it carefully and get a written estimate before authorizing the repairs to be done. Make sure time and financial constraints are clearly communicated in advance to the shop. Once repairs are complete, get an itemized list of all work. Clear communication could help eliminate potential problems. Once the work is done, pay the bill. A common situation arises when a bill goes unpaid, the shop can file a mechanic's lien which allows the shop to keep possession of the vehicle until the bill is paid. If enough time elapses, they may even take ownership and have title transferred to them in order to collect the debt.

DRIVER'S LICENSE SUSPENSIONS

Your Texas driver's license may be either suspended or revoked for a lot of different reasons. Alcohol-related suspensions make up the vast majority of situations as discussed in the DWI section in Chapter 6, but there are others. Driver's license suspensions have become increasingly popular as a deterrent for other behavior related to driving or not, especially in all drug cases and for minors convicted of alcohol-related crimes. Because the Texas and U.S. Supreme Court have determined that driving is not a right, but a privilege, states can closely and increasingly regulate driver's licenses in almost any manner they see fit. Automatic driver's license suspensions occur upon a conviction and subsequent report by the convicting court to the DPS of the conviction. The length of the suspension depends on the type of conviction and the person's history. Below is a summary of automatic and other discretionary suspensions, but does not include every possibility.

CONVICTION OF A CRIME

A person's license is automatically suspended upon final conviction for: Criminally Negligent Homicide (involving a vehicle); Evading Arrest or Detention; DWI; Intoxication Assault; Intoxication Manslaughter; Failure to Stop and Render Aid (involving injury or death); Possession/Display or Fictitious or Altered Driver's License; Permit Another to Possess Yours; Possess Multiple Driver's Licenses; Fraudulently Attempt to Obtain a Fictitious Driver's License; any Felony Traffic Code Offense; any drug offense; and Driving While their License is under Suspension, revocation, or cancellation (DWLS). If your license is from another state and has been suspended, you are not eligible for the issuance of a Texas license and if something happens in another state while you have a Texas driver's license, the Texas license is subject to suspension and/or cancellation upon receipt of a notice of conviction of an offense committed in another state that, if committed in this state, would cause a suspension. A person who does not hold a Texas Driver's License at the time of conviction is prohibited from getting a Texas Driver's License for 180 days and this prohibition period does not begin until the person makes contact with DPS for the issuance of a driver's license or reinstatement.

TOO MANY SPEEDING & TRAFFIC TICKETS

A person who receives four or more moving violations in a period of twelve months, or seven or more moving violations in a period of twenty-four months, is subject to having their license suspended, as is anyone convicted of two or more violations of a driver's license restriction/endorsement, such as driving without corrective lens or outside of certain hours.

INSURANCE PROBLEMS & ACCIDENTS

If you are convicted of a second offense for no liability insurance, your license is subject to a suspension that is indefinite, until you file and maintain proof of financial responsibility (i.e. SR-22). If DPS receives notice that a person has cancelled their insurance while required to maintain an SR-22, suspension will re-occur.

The Student Body of Law

If DPS receives notice that a person has been involved in an accident that occurred on a public street or highway, which resulted in injury, death or property damages of at least $1,000.00, the uninsured driver that caused the damage is subject to license suspension. In order to get this type of suspension lifted, you must either: provide evidence of liability insurance at the time of the accident; pay for the damages and secure a full and final liability release; or file an executed installment agreement; or file a security deposit with the State along with an SR-22. If there are no civil suits pending or unpaid judgments two years after the date of the accident, you can get your license reinstated. If there is an unsatisfied judgment arising out of a traffic accident that occurred on a public street or highway, the driver's license of the person who the judgment is rendered against is subject to suspension.

DELINQUENT CHILD SUPPORT PAYMENTS
The Texas Attorney General's office is authorized to obtain an order for DPS to suspend and revoke a person's driver's license for delinquent child support payments. The license will be revoked until the Attorney General's office or a court orders DPS to reinstate the license.

MEDICAL REASONS
When someone applies for or renews their driver's license and they provide medical information that calls into question a person's ability to safely operate a motor vehicle, or when DPS is notified by a family member, a physician, or any citizen about a license holder that they think has some medical condition that prevents them from safely driving, an investigation may begin that may result in a request for medical information by the MAB. The Texas Department of Health governs the Medical Advisory Board (MAB), which is a panel of physicians that reviews the medical condition of a person to make sure they can safely operate a car. The review may be based on medical documentation submitted by the individual's personal physician regarding the medical condition in question. If the MAB determines that a person cannot safely drive due to their medical condition, DPS will enforce the decision by revoking that person's driver's license. There are three basic types of medical revocations:
1) Revoked Incapable (driver must be medically approved by the Medical Advisory Board to lift revocation);
2) Revoked MAB No-Reply (driver must submit current medical informa-

tion to the Medical Advisory Board to lift revocation); and

3) Revoked Test Required (driver must pass the written and/or driving exam to lift revocation).

REINSTATEMENT

If your license has been suspended for any reason, such as habitual violations, medical reasons, DWI, DUI under 21 or certain criminal convictions, upon the expiration of the suspension period, you must file with the DPS for reinstatement of your license by sending them a reinstatement form and a reinstatement fee, usually $125.00. Adults convicted of a drug offense are required to complete a drug education program and minors have educational requirements as well. A certificate of completion must be forwarded to DPS. If you have any questions about what you must do for reinstatement, call DPS-Driver Improvement and Control at (512) 424-2600. DPS may also require the filing of an SR-22 as a pre-requisite to a license suspension being lifted or the license reissued, renewed, or reinstated. See the above-section about insurance for a more detailed explanation of SR-22.

CLEARING-UP OUT-OF-STATE PROBLEMS

In order to lift or prevent a suspension of a Texas license due to another state's notification, you will have to obtain a clear status from that state's respective driver licensing agency. Upon confirmation of the clear status from the out-of-state licensing agency, contact must be made with Texas Department of Public Safety (DPS) Headquarters at 512-424-2600 in order for the clearance/compliance to be applied to the Texas driver record. For this type of cancellation, documents submitted to DPS from an out-of-state Court are NOT acceptable as proof of compliance. Compliance must originate from that state's driver licensing agency. DPS may also revoke a driver's license if the person has not complied with the terms of a traffic citation received in another state. Proof of payment for the out of state citation must be submitted to DPS. Proof of payment includes receipt from court, copy of money order or cashiers check, or copy of cancelled check (front and back).

SPEEDING TICKETS & OTHER MOVING VIOLATIONS

One Friday after classes, the Aggie departs lovely College Station and speeds off down the highway on his way to see his girlfriend at SMU in Dallas. He sets the cruise control on his pickup at 80 mph. The DPS Trooper sees him

The Student Body of Law

come over the hill and BANG: the lights, the siren, the horror. The trooper saunters up to the window, the Aggie rolls down the window and the trooper asks, "You got any ID?" The Aggie responds, "About what?"

Everyone seems to push the envelope when traveling the highways. If you speed, be prepared to get tickets. Try to keep it within ten mph of the limit and you will reduce your chances of getting pulled over. Always travel in the right lane, unless passing, their radar guns are usually trained on the left or fast lane. If you are stopped, remember the helpful hints in Chapter Two and politely sign the ticket. You are only acknowledging you got the ticket and you agree to appear in court. There will be all the information on the ticket as far as the where and when you must appear. Arguing with the officer or demanding to see his radar will not get you anywhere but maybe the local jail.

A speeding ticket is a Class C offence, which means that you cannot be put in jail if convicted, only fined. You can, however, be arrested for Class C offenses, but are usually only issued a ticket. If you refuse to sign the ticket, the police officer has no choice but to arrest you to make sure you appear in front of a judge on the ticket. Your signature is your promise to appear in court on or before the date on the ticket.

YOUR OPTIONS

When you receive a speeding ticket or other Class C ticket, there are four basic alternatives:

1) Pay the ticket. The downside is that it will go on your record, possibly affecting your insurance rate. The upside is that it's over and done with;

2) Ask to take Defensive Driving. The downside is that it will cost you a fee to the Court; you'll have to get your driving record; take the class (eight hours); return the proof of attendance to the court and you can only take it once every year for a ticket. The upside is that it stays off your record and gives you a reduction in insurance rate;

3) Set it for Trial. Appear with or without an attorney, enter a plea of Not Guilty, and ask for a jury trial. The court will either give you a trial date or will notify you later. If you choose this route, you may want to hire an attorney. If trial day comes and the cop shows up, you will be expected to try the case in accordance with the rules of evidence and procedure, just like a lawyer. Sounds easy, but it's not and you are not familiar with the rules of evidence and questioning.

There are plenty of lawyers that specialize in traffic tickets who are reasonable and worth the money. Ask around and you'll find the lawyers that specialize in this area. The upside is that your attorney will handle everything;

4) If you have hired an attorney and have set it for trial and the cop showed up, the prosecutor may offer you Deferred Adjudication. This basically means that you will pay a reduced administrative fee and promise not to be convicted of a moving violation within a certain period of time, usually thirty to ninety days. Once that period of time period has expired, then the case is dismissed. The down-side is that you will pay the fee and have to watch yourself for the next month or so. If you don't, then it will be a conviction (see #1 above). The upside, it's dismissed.

Any effect on your driver's license is covered in the earlier section dealing with driver's license suspension issues and may arise if you continue to get tickets. Read the sections dealing with License Suspensions in Chapter Five.

DRIVER'S LICENSE POINTS & SURCHARGES

Texas has recently followed the lead of many other states in assigning points for various traffic offenses, if convicted. DPS then charges a surcharge when the license is renewed. Anyone who accumulates six or more points during the preceding 36-month period is charged $100 for the first six points and $25 for each additional point. This applies whether it occurred in Texas or another state. DPS assigns two points for each conviction for a moving violation that arises out of a separate transaction and three points for a moving violation that results in an accident.

You may ask, "what is a moving violation?" Well, Grasshopper, I'll tell you; it's whatever the DPS decides, but basically it is speeding, failure to yield, running red lights and stop signs and those types of tickets. There are some limitations, like no points assigned to a person's driver's license for speeding if it is less than ten percent faster than the posted speed limit and it's not in a school zone. Also, no points if the court places you on Deferred Adjudication or allows Defensive Driving.

A recent manifestation of this has been enacted that also allows a surcharge for certain other convictions, namely DWI or other "offense relating to the operating of a motor vehicle while intoxicated." DPS assesses a sur-

The Student Body of Law

charge on the license of each person who during the preceding 36-month period has been finally convicted of any offense "relating to the operating of a motor vehicle while intoxicated." The surcharge for a first offense is $1,000 per year; $1,500 for a second or subsequent conviction within a 36-month period. If there was a blood, breath, or urine specimen that was 0.16 or above involved in the conviction, then the surcharge is $2,000. See SHOULD I BLOW section of Chapter Six for other reasons why you should or should not give a specimen if requested. There are also surcharges of $100 if you are convicted of Driving While License is Suspended or Invalid and Failure to Maintain Financial Responsibility.

SO YOU'VE HAD AN ACCIDENT- WHAT TO DO AND NOT DO

If you have an accident, under Texas law, it is necessary for you do a couple of things or you run the risk of being charged with a crime. What you must do and when you may leave the scene of an accident depends upon the nature of the accident. Most importantly, call for medical assistance if anyone is injured and provide basic first aid to anyone injured. Leaving the scene is not an option under the law.

You and our old friend Joe are driving home from the library late one evening and Joe swerves to miss a dog that runs into the road. As a result of Joe's humanity, he accidentally side-swipes a parked car. No one is around and no one is in the car, what should Joe do?

Under Texas law, an accident that results in damage requires the driver to stop at the scene or as near as is practicable, without obstructing traffic and remain at the scene until you have given your name, address, the vehicle's registration number and insurance information, as well as show your driver's license and provide reasonable assistance to anyone injured. Therefore, Joe must stop and locate the owner of the vehicle and provide his name and address, if possible. If not, then he must leave a written note left in a conspicuous place or securely attached in a plainly visible location on the vehicle (usually under the window wiper or taped to the door window), that contains the driver's name and address and a statement of the circumstances of the collision. This also applies to situations where fixtures such as: signs, light poles, fences, mailboxes, or landscaping is damaged from an accident. If this happens and you can't find the owner, make a report to local law enforcement within ten days of the accident.

If you're involved in an accident, even a fender bender and your vehicle can be safely moved and it is blocking a main lane, ramp, shoulder, or median in a metropolitan area, you should move your vehicle to a safe area or accident investigation site, if available. It is not necessary to call the police. However if the accident resulted in death or injury and the vehicle is damaged to the extent that it cannot be safely driven, then you should immediately notify the local sheriff, constable, or city law enforcement by the quickest means of communication.

If no law enforcement officer comes to the scene and the accident resulted in death, injury or damage apparent to exceed $1,000.00 then you must make a written report of the accident within ten days of the accident with local law enforcement.

Anytime an officer arrives at the scene of an accident, it's a good idea to get the officer's full name and agency. Ask the officer when the accident report will be filed, its case number and how to get a copy.

Take careful notes of the date and time of the accident, the street(s) and city, the weather and road conditions, the direction and speed you and other drivers were going, a brief description of how the accident occurred, and record the license plate, driver's license, and insurance information numbers of each driver involved, as well as names, addresses, and phone numbers of any witnesses available.

If no law enforcement officer comes to the scene and the accident resulted in death, injury or damage apparent to exceed $1,000.00 then you must make a written report of the accident within ten days of the accident with local law enforcement.

CYA

Make sure you cover yourself. If the other driver is hesitant to give you their insurance information or suggests that "let's keep the insurance companies out of it, I'll just pay for the repairs," be careful. You can definitely agree to handle the repairs this way, but get their information just in case they have a change of heart after they get home and discuss it over with their wife or husband.

FILING AN INSURANCE CLAIM

After you have suffered through the accident itself and exchanged information and done everything you should, are you and your passengers okay? If you've

The Student Body of Law

been injured, even if you think that your neck is a little stiff or your knee or back is bruised, GO SEE A DOCTOR. These types of injuries can take a little while, even days to manifest their true magnitude. If these injuries persist or intensify, contact a reputable attorney to discuss how you should proceed to get the medical treatment you need. Depending on the insurance you or the other drivers have, depending on whose fault it was, you may have to work with them to receive the compensation necessary to cover your medical bills and an attorney can assist you in either pursuing a claim or guiding you through the claims process.

Now you need to get your car fixed and you need to file a claim with the insurance company to get it fixed. Phone your insurance agent or a local company representative immediately. Do it as soon as possible, even if you're far from home and even if someone else caused the accident. Ask your company or agent how to proceed and what forms or documents will be needed to support your claim, such as medical and auto repair bills and a copy of the police report. They will most likely advise you to contact the other driver's insurance company to file a claim with their insurance, if it was their fault. Keep records of your expenses because any expenses you incur as a result of the accident may be reimbursed, such as medical expenses, lost wages, or a part of your costs if you have to hire a temporary housekeeper if the injuries are that serious. Keep copies of your paperwork and supply the information your insurer needs. Normally, written notice of the accident or loss must be given to your insurance company as soon as it is reasonably possible. The notice should include: your name; names and addresses of all persons involved; date, time, place and all facts of the accident and damage; and, names and addresses of all witnesses. Cooperate with your insurance company in its investigation, settlement, or defense of any claim and turn over to the company immediately copies of any legal papers you receive in connection with your loss, but make sure you keep the originals. Your insurer will represent you if a claim is brought against you and they will attempt to settle the claim or defend you if you're sued.

It's the same as any other type of car repair, so make sure you get a complete written estimate from more than one shop. You do not have to choose the cheapest quote, but it will give you a good idea of the quality of the shop and the going rate for the repairs. Usually, the insurance company will give you a list of shops that they use. Again, you do not have to use these shops and can demand that a shop of your choosing do the repairs, but the repairs must be similar to those estimates from several shops. If you use one of the shops the insurance company suggests, the repairs are usually a little quicker and the hassle factor is usually lower. They deal with the insurance company all the time and things just seem to move a little quicker. Don't feel that you are being pushed around, but be reasonable in your demands also.

MOTORCYCLES AND SCOOTERS

"Motorcycle" means a motor vehicle designed to propel itself with not more than three wheels in contact with the ground and having a saddle for the use of the rider. For the purposes of this section, this term includes motor driven cycles and mopeds. Technically speaking though, "Moped" means a motor-driven cycle that cannot attain a speed of more than 30mph with an engine that cannot produce more than two-brake horsepower and if an internal combustion engine, has a piston displacement of 50 cubic centimeters or less and connects to a power drive system that does not require the operator to shift gears, whereas a "Motor-driven cycle" means a motorcycle equipped with a motor that has an engine piston displacement of 250 cubic centimeters or less.

These all require a specific Class M driver's license, which may be issued to a fifteen year old that restricts the rider to a motorcycle with a piston displacement under 250cc or Moped, but the 250cc restriction may be removed upon the person's sixteenth birthday. A road test is required for the Class M license, but not for a Moped license.

For all intents and purposes, the traffic laws are the same for motorcycles, as they are for other vehicles, with exception of some equipment requirements. Otherwise, know the traffic laws and follow them just like driving a car. One exception is that single rider motorcycles are allowed to drive in lanes designated for multiple passengers such as van or carpools, buses, and other high occupancy lanes.

THE HELMET LAW

Anyone who operates or rides a motorcycle on a public street or highway must wear approved protective headgear. Any peace officer may stop and detain a person who is riding a motorcycle or even a passenger to inspect the person's protective headgear for compliance with safety standards.

The Student Body of Law

EXCEPTION

Although Texas law requires any person riding on a motorcycle to wear an approved helmet, there is an exemption, which means that a person twenty-one years old or older may be exempt from wearing a motorcycle helmet if they: 1) have successfully completed an approved motorcycle operator training course; OR 2) are covered by a health insurance plan providing the person with at least $10,000 in medical benefits for injuries incurred as a result of a motorcycle accident. For more information on the course(s) that are satisfactory under this provision, as well as the particular insurance compliance and administrative procedures for applying for such an exemption, contact Texas Department of Public Safety. Once you comply with the requirements for the helmet exemption, Texas DPS will issue a helmet exemption sticker, which is placed on the bottom-center portion of the motorcycle license plate or on the license plate mounting bracket. Helmet exemption stickers are specific to the registered motorcycle it was issued for.

ORGAN DONORS

An old joke around emergency rooms is that anyone on a motorcycle without a helmet is just an organ donor. That being said, I guess this is as good a place to talk about it as anywhere. It is also known as "Statement of Gift" and anyone who wants to be an eye, tissue, or organ donor may execute a Statement of Gift by signing and carrying a donor card to evidence the donor's intentions with respect to organ, tissue, and eye donation.

A Statement of Gift on your driver's license no longer has force and effect. God forbid you're in an accident, but it happens and if you want to be an organ donor:
1) Speak with your family about your decision to donate and make sure they know about your wish to be an organ donor;
2) Sign a Uniform Donor Card, and have two family members sign the card as witnesses; and,
3) Carry the card in your wallet at all times.

If you haven't told your family you're an organ and tissue donor – you're not! If you're in an accident and you die, the doctors and hospital personnel will ask your family members for their consent to donate your organs and tissues. This is a very difficult time for any family and knowing your wishes will help make this decision easier for them and they will be much more likely to follow your wishes if you have talked to them about it.

BICYCLES

Texas defines a "Bicycle" as a device that a person may ride and that is propelled by human power and has two tandem wheels at least one of which is more than fourteen inches in diameter and typically includes a moped. This definition differentiates a bicycle from a car, or in legal lingo a "motor vehicle", which is what the traffic laws are intended to cover.

In our modern age, there are lots of devices that may or may not be considered motor vehicles or other such vehicles, so I am including the definitions of the following for reference:

1. "Motor-driven Cycle" means a motorcycle equipped with a motor that has an engine piston displacement of 250 cubic centimeters or less;
2. "Motor Vehicle" means a self-propelled vehicle or a vehicle that is propelled by electric power from overhead trolley wires;
3. "Electric Bicycle" means a bicycle that: A) is designed to be propelled by an electric motor, exclusively or in combination with the application of human power; B) cannot attain a speed of more than twenty miles per hour without the application of human power; and, C) does not exceed a weight of 100 pounds.

The traffic laws of Texas apply generally to bicycles as well, which means that a cyclist must abide by the rules of the road, just as if they were driving a car and applies to the operation of a bike on a highway; public street; or a path set aside for the exclusive operation of bicycles. The flip-side is that a bicycle has as much right to the road as a car.

There are some other rules that cyclist must abide by, such as:

1. A person operating a bicycle shall ride only on or astride a permanent and regular seat attached to the bicycle;
2. A person may not use a bicycle to carry more persons than the bicycle is designed or equipped to carry;
3. A person operating a bicycle may not use the bicycle to carry an object that prevents the person from operating the bicycle with at least one hand on the handlebars of the bicycle;
4. A person operating a bicycle, coaster, sled, or toy vehicle or using roller skates may not attach either the person or the bicycle, coast

The Student Body of Law

er, sled, toy vehicle, or roller skates to a streetcar or vehicle on a roadway;

5. A cyclist on a roadway who is moving slower than the other traffic on the roadway shall ride as near as practicable to the right curb or edge of the roadway, unless:
   - a) the person is passing another vehicle moving in the same direction;
   - b) the person is preparing to turn left at an intersection or onto a private road or driveway; or
   - c) a condition on or of the roadway, including a fixed or moving object, parked or moving vehicle, pedestrian, animal, or surface hazard prevents the person from safely riding next to the right curb or edge of the roadway.

6. A person operating a bicycle on a one-way roadway with two or more marked traffic lanes may ride as near as practicable to the left curb or edge of the roadway;

7. Persons operating bicycles on a roadway may ride two abreast. Persons riding two abreast on a laned roadway shall ride in a single lane. Persons riding two abreast may not impede the normal and reasonable flow of traffic on the roadway. Persons may not ride more than two abreast unless they are riding on a part of a roadway set aside for the exclusive operation of bicycles; and,

8. A person may not operate a bicycle unless the bicycle is equipped with a brake capable of making a braked wheel skid on dry, level, clean pavement.

There are some special rules for nighttime that require a bike to have the following:

1. a lamp on the front of the bicycle that emits a white light visible from a distance of at least 500 feet in front of the bicycle; and

2. on the rear of the bicycle:
   a) a red reflector that is:
      i.) of a type approved by the department; and
      ii.) visible when directly in front of lawful upper beams of motor vehicle headlamps from all distances from 50 to 300 feet to the rear of the bicycle; or a lamp that emits a red light visible from a distance of 500 feet to the rear of the bicycle.

TURNING SIGNALS (Hand & Arm signals)

Remember these from bike safety awareness day in elementary school? Use them. It's courteous and may keep you rolling instead of rubbing the asphalt.
1) to make a left turn signal, extend hand and arm horizontally;
2) to make a right turn signal, extend hand and arm upward, except that a bicycle operator may signal from the right side of the vehicle with the hand and arm extended horizontally; and
3) to stop or decrease speed, extend hand and arm downward.

PARKING BIKES

You can park your bike on a sidewalk so long as it doesn't impede the normal and reasonable movement of pedestrian or other traffic on the sidewalk.

CHAPTER TEN
CREDIT CARDS, BANKS & "HOT" CHECKS

THE DARK TRUTH

Whether you realize it or not, you are experiencing changes in your life at an accelerated pace right now. Away from home, really controlling your life for the first time, maybe far from home, true freedom. One thing that you are seeing a lot of, whether you realize it or not, is credit card marketing. As a matter of fact, you have probably just bought this book at the friendly campus bookstore, who not only overcharged you on this semester's books, supplies, and sweatshirt, but have also shoved credit card offers down your throat by placing flyers in your bags when you check out. Just as weird are the credit card marketing firms just hanging out on campus, at sporting events and even spring break booths giving away T-shirts, compact discs, videos, beer mugs, and more. Think about it, a free compact disc or T-shirt just to sign-up, for nothing, why not?

If you haven't realized by now, you are a prime target for the corporate consumer-based society engrossed with capitalism (the making of money) and consumerism (the spending of money). You are going to be the educated, upper-middle class that consumes a vast majority of the world's resources, which is exactly why the credit industry will want your business. In your very near future, you will rarely pay for products with cash and are soon to become an important cog in the consumerism machinery, if you let them. In order to set their hooks in you early, the marketing companies want you to sign and spend. Notwithstanding the reasonable reality that a person should have an income that well exceeds their spending to rationalize the need for a credit card. Not to mention the complete absence of any advice or education on the responsible use of a credit card and its advantages and most importantly its disadvantages, this is what I'm trying to do here.

The extreme advantage these corporations have is that most of you have not been educated on the harsh reality of credit. A recent Fannie Mae Foundation report stated that 78% of college students have a credit card, an

11% increase from 1998. The same report showed that the average college student is about $3,000 in debt, not including their student loans.

The banks and credit card companies don't even care if you max out your cards. Hell, they want you to do it. Why? Because they know what happens when you max out your card and you are desperate. "Hello Mom & Dad? Can you send me some money?" or you get a good job and ultimately pay down the debt after they have been sucking the interest out of you for years. They also know that most people keep their first credit card for an unbelievably long period of time and they also know when you get out of college and start making good money, you'll one day use it to buy a plasma flatscreen TV, a new computer, cell phones, travel, or maybe even a down payment on your new Mercedes.

Maybe your university should be required to provide a short informative lecture about credit during orientation, but they don't. College students graduate with degrees in business and finance year after year, ironically with a large chunk of credit card debt. These former students will probably struggle for years to either pay off the debt or repair their credit at a time when they really need good credit to get their lives going, like buying a new car, a house, and other things that seem to come up in the years following college. Granted, you are not worried about those things now, but believe me, your credit, especially bad credit will follow you around like an annoying little brother for a long time and worse, and will keep you from enjoying the life you have spent many years trying to achieve.

One day, in desperate need for a clean T-shirt, our old friend Joe finds himself walking through the Quad one winter day. He stops and fills out the painless and harmless application. Walking away from the table, with a clean T-shirt in his backpack, he thinks nothing of it and goes about his business. A couple of weeks later, guess what appears in Joe's dorm mailbox? A brand new shiny plastic card, with a modest credit limit. Spring Break is bearing down and Joe's bank account has all but vanished. Then the words that you heard from the marketing rep at the table weeks ago come to mind, "You'll need a credit card for travel. Where are you going on Spring Break this year? Padre Island? Skiing in Aspen?" Now Joe actually can go and his brain practically makes him think someone else is paying for the trip. Joe tells himself, just the essentials: hotel, food, and partying.

Spring Break was great. True to himself, Joe only charged the essentials, but when the bill comes in, he forgot about the tab at the bar that night he met that

The Student Body of Law

girl and her friends, not to mention the new surfboard and the small cash advance he needed to fund the last night's after hours party in the condo. Let's say Joe only spent $500 on Spring Break, but to make it through the rest of the semester, only a couple of months, go to a few parties, Joe stops at the ATM for cash advances on his credit card because his checking account is still low, maybe even buy some beer, food, and gas at the local 7-11. Even if Joe's credit card has 9% APR, many credit cards charge a much larger APR, like 19.3 % on cash advances. Many also have a 2% fee on top of the amount you withdraw.

Lets see how it's working out for Joe. Joe ambles along paying the minimum payment and then next year, while Joe's paying four times what he should be paying for his books, the friendly campus bookstore slips another credit card application in his bag at the register. Wow, another card, let's apply because the other one's filled up from Spring Break, cash advances, clothes, CD's, whatever. Joe's graduating next May and he'll get a good job and BANG, payoff the credit cards, easy.

Instead of paying off the credit Joe has now, he's opening the floodgates on another line of credit. Joe is starting to learn the intricacies of personal finance now and how to make money magically appear where there is none. Every now and then Joe bounces a few checks to the credit card company, because he was playing the float game. Now Joe's bank slaps him with a $30 overdraft penalty from time to time and your credit card tacks on the $30 late fee. These fees are now adding up to more than the entire monthly minimum payment. Joe is now paying over $100 a month just in late fees on his cards, and doesn't notice that it's piling up. Minimum monthly payments don't even keep up with all the late fees and by the way, bounced checks end up in your credit report, which we will talk about a little later. Remember the annoying little brother? He may prevent you from opening a checking account in the future or get the new car you were hoping to reward yourself with after graduation. Now at this point your saying, this guy's crazy, he has no idea who I am, Joe's an idiot. Even smart people can get caught up in this mess. It's called deficit spending. Think about it, this is the same spending philosophy that the US Government practices, which has resulted in the largest spending deficit in our country's history. Spend now, pay later. This is exactly the pattern that college students every year fall into resulting in many owing $3000 - $8000 when they graduate.

Too many people under the age of twenty-five are filing for personal bankruptcy to clear off their debts that originated while they were in college.

Bankruptcy is not a magic wand to make creditors go away; those debts stay on your credit history for ten years, while other items stay on your history for seven years. Some experts may tell you to go to your parents for advice on credit and if your parents have finance degrees, this makes sense. Unfortunately, many bankruptcies are from people in the same age group as your parents who got into debt problems in college and never got out. Seek advice from an expert, maybe even a professor in the finance department or a local banker. Be wary of credit doctors they are usually just one more person trying to take advantage of your situation.

Only use the credit cards in an emergency. Running out of beer on Friday night is not an emergency

What can be done about the epidemic of bad debt with college students? The answer is responsible spending. Only use the credit cards in an emergency. Running out of beer on Friday night is not an emergency. Try to seek financial aid to pay for books and tuition before just putting them on your credit card and never pay just the minimum payment or it will take several years to pay off your balance due to the high interest rate.

"THE DARK TRUTH BE DAMNED, I NEED A CREDIT CARD"

Okay so you still need or want a credit card. Be smart and follow the advice above and you should be okay, but one credit card is enough for a college student. There's no reason at all for you to have more than one card. If you think you need another credit card, that's the first red flag that you have a credit problem. Do you think any of the aggressive marketers on campus will tell you that?

TWO BASIC TYPES - SECURED AND UNSECURED

Unsecured credit cards are the ones that most people are familiar with. They are unsecured because they are not secured because there is no collateral attached to the debt that is extended. The credit card company is extending credit without any real protection. You see them aggressively advertised everywhere, TV, Internet SPAM, billboards, magazines, and are really aimed at people with less than perfect credit, or none at all, YOU. Because the cred-

The Student Body of Law

it card is unsecured, there may be an annual fee or a higher interest rate than regular credit cards. This is how the banks cover some of the risk associated with offering cards to people with poor or no credit history. A normal credit card is usually not advertised as non-secured, but you usually have to have a good credit rating to get them.

Be extremely cautious or just plain stay away from "secured" credit cards. Many are scams, or have such ridiculous conditions that it should alert you to staying away. Many require that you have to have money in the bank to cover them or can only be used to buy their overpriced, crappy products from their catalogue. If your credit is really that bad you should maybe reconsider getting yet another card and more debt. Go cold turkey until you get your debt under control.

The APR on department store credit cards is usually 18-21%, and most people don't bother to notice that it's much higher than their MasterCard or VISA, which is 5-15% typically. The stores entice you by giving 10% off today's purchase and you can just pay it off in full so you don't get the interest. The reality of this is consumers rarely pay it off in full when the bill comes and then they're paying 18% APR.

TRICKS TO AVOID CREDIT CARD FEES

Once you get your credit card and you normally pay your bills on time, but one month something happened and you were a little late, BANG, there appears the dreaded late fee. Call up your credit card company and ask them if they'll remove the late fee. If it's your first time, they usually will after they give you a ten second lecture about the importance of sending your payment seven days in advance to allow for snail mail. If they don't give in, threaten to close your account and transfer your balance to another card. They make money when you have accounts with balances each month. The last thing that they will want to do is lose you if you normally pay on time. Same goes for the annual fees. Call up the credit card company and tell them that you have many other cards, which don't charge annual fees. Tell them that unless they remove the annual fee you will cancel your account or transfer the balance to another card. If they really want your business, they'll cave. If not, be ready to cancel the account. You should never have to pay an annual fee, you pay enough in interest, but if you have credit problems or a history of late payments more than once, you may not have a chance with this one. It's still worth a try.

I HAVE SOMEONE ELSE'S CREDIT CARD

If you found it, call the credit card company or bank immediately. They will most-likely advise you to destroy it or send it to them. If someone gave you a card with express authorization to make a transaction, only make the transaction authorized. If you are tempted to make a charge or two without proper authorization, DON'T. Abuse of a Credit or ATM Card, better known as fraud is a State Jail Felony for each transaction. More serious offenses may be charged if the transactions are approved and property is transferred.

HOT CHECKS
SOMEONE WROTE YOU A "HOT" CHECK

If someone has written you a "hot" check, there are several options. You could just blow it off, but this not usually an acceptable option, unless of course you don't mind them stealing your money. If a check is returned by the bank marked Insufficient Funds ("ISF") and you still want to get paid, you must send a letter to the person who wrote the check, by certified mail and regular mail giving the check writer ten days to make the check good. Do not threaten criminal prosecution, simply indicate that the referenced check has been returned by the bank marked "insufficient funds" and you are making a demand for payment in full for a check that has been returned ISF. Furthermore, that if payment is not made in ten days after the date of receipt of the letter in the form of cash, money order, or cashier's check, the failure to pay creates a presumption for committing an offense and this matter may be referred for criminal prosecution. If the check is not paid within the ten days, contact the County or District Attorney's Office to obtain, prepare and deliver an Affidavit for filing criminal charges, along with a copy of the letter, the certified mail receipt (or the returned letter) and the "hot check" to the County or District Attorney's Office. A demand letter will most likely be sent requesting payment and if the "hot check" writer answers, but is unable to pay the check in full, a payment plan may be negotiated to collect the check amount and associated fees. This takes months to complete and you will not be sent a check until full payment is made to the County Attorney's Office. If the "hot check" writer does not answer, criminal charges are filed and an arrest warrant is issued. Once arrested, the prosecuting attorney will again attempt to obtain payment, usually without formal probation, but it certainly may included probation or even jail time, depending on the severity of the offense, amount of the check, the person's criminal history, and other factors.

The Student Body of Law

YOU WRITE A "HOT" CHECK

It's Friday night, and you are having a couple of beers with your girlfriend, roommates and your old buddy Joe, watchin' the tube. A pizza sounds soooo freakin' good, but last you looked, no funds in the checking account and everyone else is broke. Joe convinces you that a pizza is worth whatever trouble a "hot check" may cause, and you decide what the hell and you pick up the phone and call in the order. The delivery arrives and you scribble out the check and no worries, pizza time for everyone. There are probably lots of different reasons for writing a "hot" check, one of which is an honest mistake, but otherwise they usually fit into one of the following categories:

1. I don't have the money in the bank right now. BANG, bounced check. The pizza place will charge you a fee for the "hot" check; the bank will charge you a fee for the overdraft or returned check fee; and you run the risk of being charged with Theft by Check, the seriousness of the charge depending on how expensive the pizza was. That pizza has now cost you well over $100.
2. The money won't be in the bank 'till Monday. Pressing your luck, now your floating checks, which is not only risky, but technically a crime if you write a check knowing you don't have funds in the account to cover the check. If the pizza check clears before the deposit is credited, BANG, refer to No. 1 above, "hot" check.
3. I'll just write a check on another account and deposit it on Monday to cover this one. Brilliant idea, but similar to No. 2. BANG, now that's "check kiting". This is a form of bank fraud and depending on the amounts, may peak the curiosity of the local DA and maybe even the FBI, if you get into a scheme big enough to warrant their attention and take it to another level of criminal activity; OR
4. That account has been closed for years; they'll never find me. Yeah, right; old bank records, your old address, TDL, and other identifiers will eventually catch-up with you, probably when you are about to land that sweet job offer that comes after graduation. The background check will most likely reveal the long forgotten pizza that resulting the charges being filed and warrant for arrest issued. You'd be surprised at the lengths people will go to track you down to collect a little bit of dough, even years after your unfortunate shortage of funds.

The Texas theft statutes specify several types of theft, each with its own definition and punishment range, but "Theft by Check" specifically involves purchasing goods or services by passing a check with knowledge that the bank account is closed or has insufficient funds to cover the check. The level of offense depends on the amount of the check, over $50 makes it a Class B Misdemeanor and goes up from there.

CHAPTER ELEVEN
Traveling Abroad

TOP TEN TRAVEL TIPS FOR STUDENTS
1. Make sure you have a signed, valid passport and visas, if required. Also, before you go, fill in the emergency information page of your passport!
2. Read the Consular Information Sheets (and Public Announcements or Travel Warnings, if applicable) for the countries you plan to visit.
3. Leave copies of your itinerary, passport data page, and visas with family or friends at home, so that you can be contacted in case of an emergency. Keep your host program informed of your whereabouts.
4. Make sure you have insurance that will cover your emergency medical needs (including medical evacuation) while you are overseas.
5. Familiarize yourself with local laws and customs of the countries to which you are traveling. Remember, while in a foreign country, you are subject to its laws!
6. Do not leave your luggage unattended in public areas and never accept packages from strangers.
7. While abroad, avoid using illicit drugs, drinking excessive amounts of alcoholic beverages, and associating with people who do.
8. Do not become a target for thieves by wearing conspicuous clothing and expensive jewelry and do not carry excessive amounts of cash or unnecessary credit cards.
9. Deal only with authorized agents when you exchange money to avoid violating local laws.
10. When overseas, avoid demonstrations and other situations that may become unruly or where anti-American sentiments may be expressed.

WHERE DO I START?

Well, let's say it's Spring Break and over beers on the beach your buddies are talking about backpacking through Europe this summer. What should you do if you think you may join them? Start getting ready now. Passports and/or travel visas don't just fall from the sky. Governmental bureaucracy – even our own – takes time and red tape and in the days after 9/11 and the war on terrorism travel has become even more tricky.

Find out what information your school offers for students who are planning to study, travel, or work abroad.

This section has been drawn from reviewing many different resources, but a lion's share has been taken directly from information provided by the Department of State's Bureau of Consular Affairs; aimed to provide students, who are planning to travel or study abroad, with a few reminders about safety. Although most trips abroad are trouble free, being prepared will go a long way to avoiding the possibility of serious trouble.

If you do nothing else, become familiar with the basic laws and customs of the country you plan to visit and do a little research about the people, their culture, and any problems that the country is experiencing that may affect your travel plans. A little local knowledge may keep you on the road and out of a foreign jail. The Department of State publishes Background Notes on about 170 countries. These brief, factual pamphlets contain information on each country's culture, history, geography, economy, government, and current political situation. Background Notes are available at www.state.gov. Bookstores and the school library, not to mention the internet, should provide ample information about any part of the world you want to see.

Find out what information your school offers for students who are planning to study, travel, or work abroad. Many student advisors can provide you with information about studying or working abroad and may also be able to provide you with information on how to save money on transportation, lodging, hostels, and other things you might need to know.

If you are booking through a travel company, before plunking down that deposit, find out about the company/organization and what exactly it offers.

The Student Body of Law

Most private programs for vacation, study, or work abroad are reputable and financially sound, but some have been known to charge exorbitant fees, use deliberately false "educational" claims and describe working conditions that turn out to be far from the truth. Don't get taken, if you can help it.

Consular Information Sheets also provide updated travel information on any country in the world, including their entry regulations, crime and security assessments, drug laws/penalties, road conditions, and where you can find the U.S. embassy, consulates, and consular agencies, just in case. Also check for Travel Warnings and Public Announcements, which make recommendations that may suggest U.S. citizens defer travel to a country because of dangerous conditions.

Check these out at: http://travel.state.gov; Office of Overseas Citizens Services at 202-647-5225; or send a self-addressed, stamped business-size envelope to:

> Overseas Citizens Services
> Room 4811, Department of Stat
> Washington, DC 20520-4818.

PASSPORTS & VISAS

Passports are required to enter and/or depart most countries around the world. Apply for a passport as soon as possible. Some countries also require U.S. citizens to obtain visas before entering, we'll talk about that in a second.

A United States Passport is an internationally recognized travel document attesting to your identity and nationality. In essence, it is a request by our government that officials of foreign governments permit you to travel or sojourn in their territories and to afford you lawful aid and protection. Only Passport Services, Passport Agents of the Department of State, and Foreign Service posts designated by the U.S. Secretary of State have authority to grant, issue, or verify United States passports.

A passport is not required for travel by U.S. Citizens to any territory or waters, continental or insular, subject to the jurisdiction of the United States (including Puerto Rico, Guam, American Samoa and the U.S. Virgin Islands). As of January 2007, Mexico, Canada, Bahamas and several other countries close to the U.S. do require passports. A birth certificate or other proof of U.S. citizenship and proper ID is not enough. You should always check with the embassy for the countries you plan to visit or the U.S. State Department for particular travel destinations and entry requirements.

A passport and a visa are not the same and most countries require visitors who are planning to study or work abroad to obtain visas before entering. A visa is an endorsement or stamp placed by officials of a foreign country on a U.S. passport that allows the bearer to visit that foreign country. Basically, a visa is permission granted by the government of a country to a non-citizen to enter that country and to remain for a specific period of time. It is the responsibility of the traveler to obtain necessary visas, if any, before proceeding abroad. Visas can be obtained from the embassy or consulate of the countries to which the applicant wishes to travel, but don't wait until the last second. It can take weeks to get a visa.

I NEED A PASSPORT; HOW DO I GET ONE?

To obtain a passport, you need to go to an acceptance agent with two passport photographs of yourself, a certified copy of your birth certificate, and a valid form of photo identification, such as a driver's license. You will find the passport application there. The normal processing fee is $60 for adults sixteen or older and $40 for applicants younger than sixteen. Payment may be made in cash, by major credit or debit card, or by personal check for the full amount. Partial payments and credit card charges are not accepted. You will have to personally visit a post office or courthouse to apply for a passport, unless you are filing for a renewal. (See questions below on renewals.) During peak travel periods, the normal processing time ranges from four to six weeks, but if you need a passport more quickly, you may use the services of expediting agencies and the government also offers expedited service, which normally takes two to three weeks.

DO I NEED TO RENEW MY PASSPORT?

If you have already had a Passport issued and you answer yes to all of these questions, you can renew your passport
1) I can submit my most recent passport;
2) I was at least sixteen years old when my most recent passport was issued;
3) I was issued my most recent passport less than fifteen years ago;
4) I use the same name as on my most recent passport, OR, I have had my name changed by marriage or court order and can submit proper documentation to reflect my name changes.

If you do not have a copy of your birth certificate, you will have to con-

The Student Body of Law

tact the proper agency (Bureau of Vital Statistics or Health Department) in the state of your birth and order a vital record from that agency. If there is no official record of your birth, you will need to contact the proper agency (Bureau of Vital Statistics or Health Department) of your birth state. A letter will be issued to this fact, then other items can be used for proof. If you are a naturalized citizen, the original naturalization certificate must accompany the application for a passport and will be returned by the passport agency. If you are not a U.S. citizen and need a passport, you will need to contact the nearest consulate for your country.

If your passport has been lost, stolen, or mutilated, you must complete a new application, the DS-11, with new pictures, birth certificate, and affidavit of lost or stolen passport. The affidavit is form DS-64 available through acceptance agents.

If you are a convicted felon, it is entirely up to the discretion of the Passport Agency whether you can get one or not.

"THAT'S NOT MINE!"

To cap off your summer in Europe, you have a great weekend in Amsterdam. Joe suggests that the marijuana you have been smoking all weekend, legally, should not go to waste and one of you should hide it in your bag for the flight home. What could it hurt? It's just a little bit and would be great back at school. It should now begin to become clear that this is not a good idea and may result in the holder being subjected to a strip search, body cavity search, and federal or state drug charges. Even a small amount can cause big problems. It's not worth it.

This general rule applies to all foreign travel. The results can be quite similar, however foreign jails are usually much less comfortable than those here in the states. Trot down to the local blockbuster and rent *Midnight Express* for further details.

Another excellent rule to live by is to never carry anything through customs for someone else, without knowing exactly what it is. Your trusting nature could result in a very unpleasant circumstance. Again, not worth it.

"I'M IN ANOTHER COUNTRY; I'M IN TROUBLE; WHO DO I CALL?"

If you are in trouble in a remote area or run into some type of civil unrest, find the location of the nearest U.S. embassy or consulate and register with the Consular Section when you arrive, if possible. (U.S. embassy and consulate locations can be found in the country's Consular Information Sheet.) If your family needs to reach you because of an emergency, they can pass a message to you through the Office of Overseas Citizens Services at 202-647-5225, which will contact the embassy or consulate in the country where you are traveling and pass a message from your family to you. Remember consular officers cannot cash checks, lend money, or serve as your attorney, but they can, if the need arises, assist you in obtaining emergency funds from your family, help you find an attorney or medical assistance, and replace your lost or stolen passport.

CHAPTER TWELVE
Guilt by Association

This section is all about Joe's crazy ex-girlfriend, whom I will affectionately refer to as "Crazy Lola." Her name was Lola, but she was not a showgirl, nor did she have flowers in her hair. Their interesting relationship and the insane behavior she exhibits are intended to provide some examples of situations we can get caught up in by dating the wrong kind of person. These stories illustrate the fact that your date's behavior can have serious negative consequences for you. So no matter how "hot" that someone might be, cool down and think carefully about who you want to go out with.

SHE'S BEEN CAUGHT STEALING

Out for an afternoon of light shopping at the local department store, Joe wanders through the aisles picking out detergent, socks, the odds and ends of life, when he sees Lola stuff a pair of sexy underwear into her purse, and then a razor for him, and walk out the door. That's right Lola is a shoplifter  and has committed the offense of Theft. The level of offense depends on the amount of money involved or the fair market value of all items lifted in the same act. If convicted more than twice, it's a felony, no matter what is taken or how inexpensive.

SHE'S A PAPERHANGER

One day Joe notices that the beer keg, tap, and ice barrel that Lola rented for a party last month are still in her garage. He asks her about it and she says, "Don't worry; I wrote a hot check for it. I'm not taking it back." This is Theft of Service, which involves securing a service with no intent to make payment, or holding a rental item beyond the agreed upon rental period (see Chapter 10 on Hot Checks).

SHE'S LOUD

The party at Lola's apartment is going great until she decides that it's disco night, and pumps up the volume to ear-bleeding levels. This soon attracts not only complaints from neighbors, but the presence of the cops. They ask that the music be lowered, and warn everyone to quiet down.

After the cops leave, the fact that she cannot enjoy herself in the privacy of her own home seems to agitate Lola, and she responds by cranking it up and dancing on the coffee table. The cops quickly return and ask that the owner step outside to discuss the matter. She does, and BANG, she's charged with a Class C misdemeanor of Noise, and may be arrested if she gives them any attitude. Noise is presumed to be unreasonable if it exceeds 85 decibels after the person is told by the cops to turn it down. Surprise, Lola gives the cops some lip, and Joe and the others get to enjoy the rest of the party without her company. He figures he'll make her bond first thing in the morning.

SHE'S OBNOXIOUS

One evening Joe is having a few drinks down at the local bar with some friends, and in comes Lola with some of her friends. They mix and mingle and then it happens: As a joke, Joe pinches Lola on the rear in the midst of a crowd and then fades into the crowd so that Lola can't tell who did it. Although you and your buddy, were in the men's room when it happened, Lola decides that it had to be your buddy who committed the infraction. Lola confronts your buddy. He denies it, and for the next few minutes she continues to scold him anyway. She escalates to screaming profanities, not only at your buddy, but at everyone who seems to now be laughing at her display. She gives them the finger as the bouncers escort her out of the bar.

Lola committed the offense of Disorderly Conduct, which is a catchall for the local cops to use to keep order. Persons can be charged with Disorderly Conduct if an officer is informed of or witnesses their engaging in any of the following behaviors without significant provocation:

1) using abusive, indecent, profane or vulgar language, or making an offensive gesture or display in a public place, and the language or display tends to incite an immediate breach of the peace;
2) creating by chemical means a noxious and unreasonable odor in a public place;

The Student Body of Law

3) abusing or threatening a person in a public place in an obviously offensive manner;
4) making an unreasonable noise in a public place other than a sport shooting range;
5) fighting with another in a public place;
6) entering onto the property of another and, for a lewd or unlawful purpose, looking into a dwelling on the property through any window or other opening in the dwelling;
7) while on the premises of a hotel or comparable establishment, looking into a guest room not one's own through a window or other opening in the room, for a lewd or unlawful purpose;
8) discharging a firearm in a public place other than on a public road or at a sport shooting range;
9) displaying a firearm or other deadly weapon in a public place in a manner calculated to alarm;
10) discharging a firearm on or across a public road; or
11) exposing one's anus or genitals in a public place and being reckless about whether another may be present who will be offended or alarmed by the act.

SHE'S A RIOT

Wow, what a girl that Lola, full of energy and sometimes anger, especially towards authority. Her organizing the charity music festival was a great idea, and things go just fine until the cops arrive and order the crowd to disburse. In an effort to salvage the event, Lola grabs the mic and suggests that the crowd "stand up to the cops" and burn their patrol cars. The crowd responds by approaching the cop cars. As the cops drag her from the stage, Joe begins to realize that her behavior can sometimes adversely affect his well-being.

She is charged with Riot, a Class B misdemeanor. Riot is the assemblage of seven or more persons, resulting in conduct which:

1) creates an immediate danger of damage to property or injury to persons
2) substantially obstructs law enforcement or other governmental functions or services; or
3) by force, threat of force, or physical action deprives any person of a legal right or disturbs any person in the enjoyment of a legal right.

SHE'S A PROTESTER

The university has raised the tuition rates again, and Lola urges Joe to stage a protest through passive activities. As any supportive boyfriend would, Joe agrees to lie down at the intersection of Congress and 6th Streets in Austin, along with some of Lola's friends, in protest. This brings traffic to a halt and creates a huge tangle of cars and buses. Austin's finest are quickly dispatched and they ask that everyone please move out of the way. When it becomes apparent that the protesters are not going to move, the police begin to handcuff and drag them from the street. BANG, BANG, BANG, BANG, BANG. You get the picture; all are arrested for obstructing the street. The good news is that Joe has plenty of company in jail; the bad news is that this chick keeps getting him in trouble and he keeps letting it happen.

The charge of Obstructing a Highway or Other Passageway is usually used against such protesters. It is applied when, without legal privilege or authority, a person obstructs a highway, street, sidewalk, railway, waterway, elevator, aisle, hallway, entrance, or exit to which the public has access, or any other place used for the passage of persons, vehicles, or conveyances, regardless of the means of creating the obstruction; or when a person disobeys a reasonable request or order to move by a peace officer, fireman or other person with authority to control the use of the premises. It is a Class B misdemeanor.

ONE MORE PROTEST

During one of Joe and Lola's many breakups, he reads the following headline in the university rag: "City Council Meeting Halted Due to Student Protest." The article describes how an unidentified female student stood up on her seat during the council's debate on a permit for the homecoming parade that is sponsored by university Greek organizations. The student began to loudly chant, "Greeks oppress, Greeks suppress," until she was dragged from the hall by security. Knowing it had to be his crazy ex-girlfriend, Joe shakes his head and walks to class with a sigh of relief because he had broken up with her, so he doesn't have to bail her out this time. Disrupting a Meeting or Procession is the charge here. It applies to anyone who prevents

The student began to loudly chant, "Greeks oppress, Greeks suppress"

The Student Body of Law

or disrupts a lawful meeting, procession or gathering, by physical action or verbal utterance. It is a Class B misdemeanor.

SHE'S THE MAD BOMBER

Joe and Lola walk to class together for a biology exam, lamenting their lack of preparedness. Joe sits down in the classroom, but Lola excuses herself. Within a few minutes the professor comes in and instructs everyone to evacuate the building. As he walks out of the building, Joe sees Lola standing next to a pay phone and he hears a professor say that it was a bomb threat. Crazy Lola chose to commit a felony rather than properly prepare for the test.

You can be charged with False Alarm or Report if you knowingly initiate, communicate, or circulate a report of a present, past, or future bombing, fire, offense, or other emergency that you know is false or baseless and that would ordinarily: 1) cause action by an official or volunteer agency organized to deal with emergencies; 2) place a person in fear of imminent serious bodily injury; or 3) prevent or interrupt the occupation of a building, room, place of assembly, place to which the public has access, or aircraft, automobile, or other mode of conveyance. It is a Class A misdemeanor unless the false report is of an emergency involving a public primary or secondary school, public communications, public transportation, public water, gas or power supply, or other public service, in which event the offense is a state jail felony.

SHE CRIES WOLF

Joe begins to suspect that Lola is teetering on the brink. She starts to perceive even the most mundane occurrences as life threatening, usually thinking someone is trying to break into her apartment. Joe had been summoned many times to assure her that everything was okay, but because he can never find anything actually wrong, she begins to call 911. This makes her well known to the local cops. Finally, the 911 operator tells her not to call unless there is an actual emergency. Lola's response is a terse insult. When the cops arrive this time they actually arrest someone—her. Silent or Abusive Calls to 9-1-1 Service is the charge against someone who makes a telephone call to 911 when there is not an emergency, and knowingly or intentionally: 1) remains silent, 2) makes abusive or harassing statements, or 3) permits a telephone under their control to be used by another to do so. It's a Class B misdemeanor.

THE BREAKUP

There is crisis in paradise and Joe knows that their love is in trouble. One night he gets into an argument with Crazy Lola. Her dating other people had become an obstacle in their exclusive relationship, and when he confronts her about it an argument ensues. She smacks him in the face, then she starts wrecking the apartment and yelling at him. He tells her that if she doesn't calm down and stop trashing the place he is going to call the cops. In response, she grabs the phone, rips it out of the wall, and throws it out of the window.

Lola has committed the offense (among others) of Interference with an Emergency Telephone Call. This offense occurs when someone knowingly prevents or interferes with another's ability to place an emergency telephone call, or recklessly renders unusable the telephone that would be used to request assistance in an emergency from a law enforcement agency, medical facility, or other agency, or entity the primary purpose of which is to provide for the safety of individuals. She has committed a Class A misdemeanor, and it would have been a State Jail felony if she had previously been convicted for the same thing. This may also be Assault, for smacking Joe in the face and Criminal Mischief if there was damage from the phone being ripped out and thrown, or other damage to the apartment.

SHE SAID SHE'D GET HIM BACK

As she flails around the apartment throwing and breaking stuff, Lola whacks herself with the phone receiver on the side of her face. It leaves a nice mark, and Joe finds it humorous. As she leaves, she threatens to get him back.

A little later there's a knock on the door. Two police officers are standing outside and ask Joe if he is who he is. He says yes and they inform him that Lola has called them. She is claiming not only that he hit her in the face, but that she is living with him and that he has done it on numerous occasions. The cops look around and see the mess. Joe tries to explain that it was she who went nuts, but she had made the call, she had an injury that was consistent with the allegation, and she was small, cute and crying. They don't listen to Joe, and BANG, they take him to jail for Assault on a Family Member, domestic violence.

Normally, individuals are charged with a Class A misdemeanor if someone claims that they intentionally, knowingly, or recklessly caused the accuser bodily injury. The offense is elevated to a felony of the third degree if it is committed against a public servant or a member of the defendant's family or household when the person charged has been previously convicted of an

The Student Body of Law

offense against a member of his or her family. "Family" here includes related individuals, former spouses, and parents of the same child whether they reside together or not. "Household" means persons living together in the same dwelling, without regard to whether they are related to each other. This includes roommates and live-in boyfriends and girlfriends.

It will take Joe a good attorney, a chunk of cash, and a considerable amount of time to try to convince the local DA that he isn't a woman beater, and then to get the erroneous record expunged—that is, if he succeeds at all.

SHE'S A LIAR

In a surprise turnaround, the local DA sees through Lola's manipulative ways and charges her with making a False Report in relation to her rampage and self-inflicted injuries at Joe's apartment. When she called the cops and reported that Joe had assaulted her, she intended to deceive by knowingly making a false statement that was material to a criminal investigation to a peace officer conducting the investigation.

Lola was no newcomer to fibbing. She testifies at her girlfriend's DWI trial that she had been with her girlfriend all that night and had seen her drink only two beers, when she had actually seen her drink four tequila shots and four beers. Crazy Lola perjured herself. The offense of Perjury is committed when someone makes a false statement under oath or swears to the truth of a false statement previously made and the statement is either required or authorized by law to be made under oath. It is a Class A misdemeanor. In this case, the false statement is made during an official proceeding, and is material, which makes it Aggravated Perjury, a third degree felony.

In a rare moment of clarity and a stroke of good judgment, Lola retracts her false statements before completion of her testimony and before the falsity of the statements is exposed. This is the only defense to the perjury charge, other than that the statement is in fact true.

SHE'S AN ENTREPRENEUR

Lola has a little business enterprise on the side; she has a knack for making fake IDs. She will, for a small fee, either change your ID to reflect the age necessary for alcohol consumption or create a new one with the photo studio she has set up in her dorm room. She has even created a huge, proportional driver's license template on the wall. All you have to do is stand in the right spot and she takes your picture in front of the wall that looks like a huge driver's license. She develops the film and laminates your new fake ID right there, and you are ready to roll the clubs that night.

She is committing the offense of Tampering with a Government Record. This is committed anytime a person:

1) makes a false entry in, or false alteration of, a government record;
2) makes, presents or uses any record or document with knowledge of its falsity and with the intent that it be taken as a genuine government record;
3) intentionally destroys, conceals, removes, or otherwise impairs the verity, legibility, or availability of a government record;
4) possesses, sells, or offers to sell a government record or a blank government record form with the intent that it be used unlawfully;
5) makes, presents, or uses a government record with knowledge of its falsity; or
6) possesses, sells, or offers to sell a government record or a blank government record form with knowledge that it was obtained unlawfully.

Unfortunately, Lola is asked to leave college four semester-hours short of graduation. That doesn't stop her from telling the world she has a degree. Using her skills from the fake ID business, she expertly creates a transcript and diploma, even improving a couple of those grades. She uses it to get her first job, and from then on even she probably forgets that it is fake—until she applies for a government job and they actually check the records. Oops. BANG, a third degree felony of Tampering with a Government Record, or a second degree felony if she intended to defraud or harm another.

"Government Record" has a broad definition that includes anything belonging to, received by, or kept by government for information, including a court record; anything required by law to be kept by others for the information of government, including a license, certificate, permit, seal, title, letter of patent, or similar document issued by government, by another state, or by the United States; and also including proof of motor vehicle liability insurance; a certificate of an insurance company; an electronic submission or other evidence of financial responsibility; or an official ballot or other election record.

The Student Body of Law

THE BREAKUP CONTINUES

Since Lola beats Joe to the punch with her allegation of assault, which causes him months of hell, Joe succumbs to irrational thought and decides one day to send her an anonymous message in response. He pays her car a little visit in the middle of the night and in his best handwriting scratches an expletive in the door with a screwdriver. He committed the offense of Criminal Mischief, which occurs when a person intentionally damages or destroys another's tangible property without their consent, and which specifically includes markings, inscriptions, slogans, drawings, and paintings. The severity of the offense depends on the amount of monetary damage done, as follows:

1) less than $50—Class C misdemeanor
2) $50 or more but less than $500—Class B misdemeanor
3) $500 or more but less than $1,500—Class A misdemeanor
4) $1,500 or more but less than $20,000—State Jail felony
5) $20,000 or more but less than $100,000—third degree felony
6) $100,000 or more but less than $200,000—second degree felony
7) $200,000 or more—first degree felony

SHE'S NOT GONNA LET IT GO

Crazy Lola is no dummy; she knows who decorated her car, and so begins an endless string of silent phone calls, hang-ups, abusive and obscene e-mails, and threatening IMs. Her actions constitute the Class B misdemeanor offense of Harassment. This occurs when one intends to harass, annoy, alarm, abuse, torment, or embarrass another by:

1) telephone, writing or electronic communication and in the course of the communication makes a comment, request, suggestion or proposal that is obscene;
2) causing the other person's telephone to ring repeatedly or making repeated telephone communications anonymously;
3) making a telephone call and intentionally failing to hang up or disengage the connection; or
4) sending repeated electronic communications.

NOW SHE'S A STALKER

It's now getting out of control. Crazy Lola is there every time Joe leaves one of his classes. She hangs out at his apartment pool and other places that make it clear she is following him. He finds a note on his door suggesting that some unfortunate accident will soon befall him, his mother, or his dog Sparky, and maybe the stray cat that he feeds on the patio of his apartment. BANG, Joe is being stalked. This constitutes the offense of Stalking because on more than one occasion Lola followed Joe and made him fear bodily injury or death and that an offense would be committed against him, his family, or their property. His fear was reasonable under the law because her actions would cause any reasonable person to fear bodily injury to themselves or a member of their family. Stalking is a third degree felony.

SHE'S TAKING IT OUT ON THE PETS

Now for the last straw. Joe's neighbors see Lola abduct the stray cat he feeds on the porch, and it is later found on his doorstep, suffocated in a plastic bag. She has committed the Class A misdemeanor of Cruelty to Animals by torturing and killing the cat. Cruelty to animals also includes:

1) failing to reasonably provide necessary food, care or shelter for an animal in the person's custody;
2) unreasonably abandoning an animal in the person's custody;
3) transporting or confining an animal in a cruel manner;
4) seriously injuring or administering poison to an animal, other than cattle, horses, sheep, swine or goats, belonging to another without legal authority or the owner's effective consent;
5) causing one animal to fight with another;
6) using a live animal as a lure in dog-race training or in dog coursing on a racetrack;
7) tripping a horse; and
8) seriously overworking an animal.

HER EAST-TEXAS COUSIN, THE ANIMAL LOVER

Before the big breakup, while Joe is visiting Crazy Lola's family in East Texas, her cousin invites him out for a beer with the boys. After a few cool ones, Joe finds himself bouncing down a long dirt road to a barn. There is quite a crowd. Joe asks what's going on, but Cousin Carl and his buddies only chuckle and say, "You'll see." As they get closer to the barn Joe hears dogs barking. He looks through the crowd and he sees a ring, stained with blood. Inside the ring are two pissed-off dogs being held apart by two rednecks. About that time the cops arrive and Joe is one of the first people arrested. He later learns that even the spectators are committing the offense of Dog Fighting. A person

The Student Body of Law

commits this offense if he intentionally:

1) causes a dog to fight with another dog, for money or not;
2) participates in the earnings of or operates a facility used for dog fighting;
3) uses or permits another to use any real estate, building, room, tent, arena, or other property for dog fighting;
4) owns or trains a dog with the intent that the dog be used in an exhibition of dog fighting; or
5) attends as a spectator an exhibition of dog fighting.

The spectators are charged with a Class C misdemeanor; the trainers and handlers are charged with a Class A misdemeanor; and the owners of the barn and anyone else that profited are charged with a state jail felony.

SHE'S STILL PROTESTING

Years after graduation, after two wives, two weddings and one bankruptcy, Joe is watching the nightly local news. The talking heads mention a protest that resulted in several arrests. The reporter can be seen with a crowd in the background, and as the camera gets closer, jiggled by the crowd, Joe sees the subject of the story. There she is, Crazy Lola, torching Old Glory in the name of whatever cause she is supporting or denouncing at the time. He thanks God that he extracted himself from her way back when.

A person commits the Class A misdemeanor offense of Destruction of Flag if they intentionally damage, deface, mutilate, or burn the flag of the United States or of the state of Texas. It must be an actual flag, not just a representation of a flag on a piece of paper, clothing or other object or material.

A person commits the Class A misdemeanor offense of Destruction of Flag if they intentionally damage, deface, mutilate, or burn the flag of the United States or of the state of Texas. It must be an actual flag, not just a representation of a flag on a piece of paper, clothing or other object or material.

CHAPTER THIRTEEN
JUST FOR THE WOMEN

(This chapter was written for women, in the hope that it will provide insight into some practical and legal issues that are specific to a woman's experience.)

GIRLS GONE WILD

Joe's sister, Sissy, who is remarkably similar to Joe and shares many of the same gene-pool characteristics, heads down to Padre for spring break with some girlfriends, right on the heels of their trip to Bourbon street during Mardi Gras a couple of weeks before. They find the party scene on Padre very similar: mobs of alcohol-soaked kids, cheap beer, public urination, and even "bead-baiting," which they had become quite adept at. Sissy and her girls are coaxed into showing their goods after they have a few beers and a few shots. Fortunately, none of them are busted for their public baring of breasts, and they assume all is well.

Later that semester, Sissy happens upon some guys in the frat house watching a video of girls exposing themselves during spring break. To her shock, she sees her whole gang shaking their goods on the beach at Padre. Someone is not only showing it to the world, but making lots of money doing it.

Some have filed lawsuits challenging the use, sale, and distribution of such videos. A herein unnamed twenty-five year old former swimsuit model in Florida discovered that she was a "Girl Gone Wild—Sexy Sorority Sweetheart," and filed a lawsuit claiming to have been an unwitting and unwilling participant in the use of her likeness, and that the video resulted in her being subjected to ridicule and embarrassment. Others have tried also, to no avail.

You need to know that there are people who send camera crews out to wander the beaches and streets of spring break, Mardi Gras, and campus parties looking for opportunities to record spontaneous and usually drunken young women flashing their breasts during those fun-filled events. Producers of the "Girls Gone Wild" videos, and others, offer videos for sale of young women baring it all, usually in public places. These videos are marketed on the

The Student Body of Law

Internet and in late-night TV infomercials, resulting in unbelievable profits for their producers. Reports have estimated that the Girls Gone Wild empire clears over $100 million annually, and they don't owe a dime of it to the girls. Now for the kicker—it's all legal.

Do you have a right to privacy in public areas? Generally speaking, no. So, no matter how many beers, shots, and Bourbon Street hurricanes you guzzle down, you should not forget that someone in the crowd may have a camera (or camera phone), and you could become tomorrow's Internet queen.

SEX

Our society has failed to adequately socialize boys and girls about how to treat each other and about what is and is not acceptable behavior. This has led to some common misbeliefs by both sexes. All too often, men view women as either virtuous or loose, and nothing in between; therefore, men are confused when it comes to interpreting the sexual desires of women. Men usually interpret flirtatious behavior as leading them on, giving them the green light to become more sexually aggressive. And a common misbelief of women is that men are more knowledgeable than they are about sex, and thus that they should defer to the man's lead.

The basic lesson here: "Say what you mean and mean what you say."

Uncertainties and misbeliefs go uncorrected because both sexes remain reluctant to express their feelings to the other sex. Even when crying, slamming doors, or rolled eyes prompt the question, "What's wrong?" the most common response is, "Nothing," instead of expressing true feelings. The verbal response doesn't match the physical behavior, thus confusing the other. This confusion and lack of communication spills over into sexual situations.

The basic lesson here: "Say what you mean and mean what you say." Do not be afraid to express yourself. It will reduce the risk of misunderstanding, embarrassment, and humiliation in those uncomfortable situations that have progressed to the point that no other options but sex seem possible. Speaking openly will spill over into other aspects of relationships and create freer and more fulfilling relationships—sexual and otherwise.

Having sex is about making choices; it comes with responsibilities and potentially with life-changing consequences. One of the great joys of life can be having a baby—when you are ready and are able to provide the love, care and support a child needs. One of the great setbacks in life can be an unintended pregnancy—especially for a young woman.

BIRTH CONTROL

According to some estimates, eighty-five percent of women who use no contraceptive during vaginal intercourse become pregnant each year. The only absolute guarantee against pregnancy is not having vaginal intercourse, but there are numerous contraceptive methods that greatly reduce that risk. FDA-approved birth control methods include condoms, diaphragms, birth control pills, Depo-Provera injections, IUDs (intrauterine devices), cervical caps, and fertility awareness methods. Ask your doctor or family planning counselor for advice if you are sexually active or are considering becoming so.

RAPE

A person commits the offense of Sexual Assault (rape) if the person intentionally:

1) causes penetration of the anus or sexual organ of another person by any means without that person's consent;
2) causes penetration of the mouth of another person by the sexual organ of the actor, without that person's consent; or
3) a third person causes the sexual organ of another person to contact or penetrate the mouth, anus, or sexual organ of another person without that person's consent.

Although sexual assault is understood as a crime of violence, it becomes "aggravated" if the perpetrator causes bodily injury; attempts to cause the death of the victim or another person in the course of the same criminal episode; places the victim in fear that death, serious bodily injury, or kidnapping will be imminently inflicted on any person; in the presence of the victim threatens to cause the death, serious bodily injury, or kidnapping of any person; uses or exhibits a deadly weapon in the course of the same criminal episode; acts in concert with another who engages in this sort of conduct; or administers or provides flunitrazepam (otherwise known as rohypnol), GHB, or ketamine (see "Date Rape Drugs" section below for more information) to the victim of the offense with the intent of facilitating the commission of the offense.

The Student Body of Law

CONSENT

"Consent" is the key to whether sex is also sexual assault. Sex is without the consent of the other person if:

1) the actor compels the other person to submit or participate by using or threatening to use physical force or violence;
2) the victim has not consented and is unconscious or physically unable to resist or is unaware that the sexual assault is occurring;
3) the actor knows that as a result of mental disease or defect the other person is at the time of the sexual assault incapable either of appraising the nature of the act or of resisting it;
4) it is coerced by a public servant, mental health service provider or clergy member by exploiting the person's emotional dependency; or
5) it is accomplished by intentionally administering any substance, without the other person's knowledge, to impair the victim's power to judge or control their own conduct.

As I said earlier to the men, "No" means no. Now to the women: you must be unequivocal when it comes to a sexual situation that you do not want to go any further. Assert yourself and your wishes, no matter what. Never put yourself in a position where there is any question in the other person's mind of whether or not what they are doing is okay with you.

WHAT DO YOU DO IF YOU HAVE BEEN SEXUALLY ASSAULTED?

Take the following steps right away if you are sexually assaulted:

1) Get away from the attacker to a safe place as fast as you can.
2) Call a friend or family member you trust, or a crisis center or hotline to talk with a counselor. One national hotline is the National Sexual Assault Hotline at (800) 656-HOPE.
3) Get counseling from a trusted professional. Feelings of shame, guilt, fear and shock are normal and need to be addressed.
4) If possible, do not wash, comb or clean any part of your body, or change clothes, so the hospital staff can collect evidence.
5) Do not touch or change anything at the scene of the assault.
6) Go immediately to the nearest hospital emergency room. You need to be examined, treated for any injuries, and screened for possible sexually transmitted diseases (STDs) or pregnancy. The hospital should collect evidence using a rape kit, including any fibers, hairs,

saliva, semen, or clothing that the attacker left behind. If they do not, tell them to do so.
7) You or the hospital staff should call the police from the emergency room to file a report.

WHAT DO YOU DO IF A FRIEND HAS BEEN SEXUALLY ASSAULTED?

First, listen to her (or him), believe her, and offer comfort. Then encourage her to take the steps detailed above, and go with her to the hospital, the police station, and counseling. Reinforce the message that it is natural to feel angry and ashamed, but that she is not at fault, and also that it is important to go forward and disclose all of the details that are asked of her.

DATE RAPE

Date rape is something that every young woman should be conscious of and protect herself from. Don't put yourself in a situation in which you do not have control. Date rape is a serious crime and can occur just as easily in casual as in serious relationships, both heterosexual and same-sex.

You are at the local campus frat party having drinks with friends and doing the things that college students do. A cute guy comes over and strikes up a conversation. You move closer to talk over the loud music. He puts his hand on your knee, and you don't say anything. You continue to talk and even flirt a little. He then puts his hand on your rear. Still, you don't say anything about his roaming hands. Instead, you suggest that you all go somewhere less crowded.

You are unwittingly putting yourself at risk. You have no way of knowing whether this guy you just met is a rapist on the prowl or just a guy looking for love. If you do not want to go down the road toward a sexual encounter, don't put yourself in a position where you can be taken advantage of. If you are not interested in sex, don't let the guy control the situation. If he does something that makes you uncomfortable, be polite and point out his indiscretion, more than once if necessary. He will perceive passivity as condoning, if not welcoming, his advances. If he continues to be aggressive, it should send up a red flag. Do not separate yourself from your friends or a crowded place. Lastly, flirtation can sometimes be interpreted as being receptive to a man's sexual advances. I am certainly not suggesting that women should never flirt, but be aware of how it may be perceived, and use caution.

The Student Body of Law

DATE-RAPE DRUGS

Alcohol and drugs are often involved in acquaintance rape or date rape. The college scene and peer group expectations on campus usually include consumption of alcohol at social events. A study of rape in Canada concluded that alcohol was used by a half of all offenders and by a third of all victims. Now date-rape drugs, such as Rohypnol, have come of age, causing even more concern. Date-rape drugs are often slipped into victims' drinks at clubs or parties without their knowing it. These drugs, as well as alcohol, can render people unable to resist assault, and leave them with a type of amnesia so that the victim is uncertain about what happened.

I want to stop here and preach a little. Just because a woman gets drunk and has sex with someone, or everyone, in the living room of the frat house does not mean that she has been sexually assaulted. Just because she is later embarrassed by her actions, and even if she took a drug that someone gave her and is now having trouble remembering the night's events, does not mean that she is the victim of sexual assault. It may simply be that she used bad judgment that night.

It is when you are unaware that you took a drug, or were tricked into it, and then are taken advantage of during a state of impairment, that you may be a victim of sexual assault. When it is without your consent, that makes it illegal. Embarrassment or humiliation later does not make a sexual act a sexual assault.

When it is without your consent, that makes it illegal

Have a good time, but be aware of what you are drinking or taking, and try to make judgments that you are prepared to accept later. Always be wary about accepting drinks from anyone you don't know well or haven't known long enough to trust. If you do accept a drink, make sure it's from an unopened container and that you open it yourself. Don't put your drink down and leave it unattended, even to go to the restroom.

The so-called date-rape drugs are abused for a number of reasons, not just for the purpose of obtaining sex. They are all illegal to possess without prescription. They usually have no color, smell, or taste, and are easily added to drinks without anyone knowing it. These drugs can cause people to become incapacitated and physically unable to protect themselves, and to have no memory of the event. They are suspected of causing health problems, and in some cases even death. Following are the main date-rape drugs:

Rohypnol
Generically called flunitrazepam, Rohypnol is prescribed as a sleeping pill outside of the United States, and is used as a short-term treatment for insomnia, as a sedative hypnotic and as a pre-anesthetic.

Street names: Rophies, Roofies, R2, Roofenol, Roche, Roachies, La Rocha, Rope, Rib, Circles, Mexican Valium, Roach-2, Roopies, Forget-Me Pill, Trip and Fall, Mind Erasers, and Ropies

Looks like: white tablets, scored on one side for breaking in half, with the word "Roche" and an encircled one or two (depending on the dosage) on the other. They are sold in pre-sealed bubble packs of one or two milligram doses. Rohypnol can be dissolved in a drink, where it is undetectable. Newer pills turn blue in liquid.

Ketamine
Ketamine is used to anesthetize animals; it is a liquid and can be made into a tablet or a powder by evaporating the liquid and reducing it to a fine white powder that can be smoked or snorted.

Street names: K, Ket, Special K, Vitamin K, Vit K, Kit Kat, Keller, Kelly's Day, Green, Blind Squid, Cat Valium, Purple, Special La Coke, Super Acid, and Super C

Looks like: clear liquid or white powder, which is often mistaken for cocaine or crystal methamphetamine

GHB (gamma-hydroxybutrate)
Originally used in psychiatric treatments, GHB has been abused in the United States for its euphoric, sedative and anabolic (bodybuilding) effects.

Street names: G, Georgia Home Boy, Liquid Ecstasy, Grievous Bodily Harm, Liquid E, GBH, Soap, Scoop, Easy Lay, Salty Water, G-Riffick, Cherry Meth, Nature's Quaalude, Zonked, Organic Quaalude, Somatomax, G, Jib, Woman's Viagra, Gamma 10, GH Buddy, Aminos, Blue Nitro, Blue Thunder, Thunder Nectar, Renewtrient, Revivarant, Remforce, Firewater, and Invigorate

Looks like: clear liquid with no odor or color, or white powder

I CAN'T REMEMBER WHAT HAPPENED; I THINK I WAS DRUGGED
If you suspect that you have been drugged without your consent, whether you think you were sexually assaulted or not, you may want to get a toxicology

The Student Body of Law

screen immediately. Popular date-rape drugs are eliminated from the body quickly and the window of opportunity to detect their presence is just a few hours. Go to your local hospital and request that blood be drawn immediately and preserved for testing. It may be needed later as evidence.

I'VE BEEN PHYSICALLY ABUSED
If you have been physically abused or threatened, you should take the following steps:
1) Leave immediately, especially if you or your children are in danger!
2) Call a local crisis hotline or the National Domestic Violence Hotline at (800) 799-SAFE or TDD (800) 787-3224; the latter is available 24/7 in English, Spanish, and other languages, and will give you the phone numbers of local hotlines and other resources;
3) Understand that you're not alone. Many women are victims of domestic abuse;
4) Don't ignore it or wait for it to go away. It won't go away;
5) Don't keep it to yourself; get help. Talk with someone: a family member, friend, colleague, or faith counselor; and
6) If you've been hurt, get medical attention, call the police and take pictures of the injuries.

SIGNS OF ABUSE
It may be embarrassing, difficult, and confusing to admit, even to yourself, that you are in an abusive relationship, but there are some clear warning signs of a potentially abusive relationship. These include a partner who:
1) Keeps track of what you are doing all the time and criticizes you for little things;
2) Constantly accuses you of being unfaithful;
3) Prevents or discourages you from seeing friends or family, or going to work or school;
4) Gets angry when drinking alcohol or using drugs;
5) Controls the money you spend;
6) Humiliates you in front of others;
7) Destroys your property or things that you care about;
8) Threatens or acts to hurt you, the children, or pets (by hitting, punching, slapping, kicking, or biting);
9) Uses or threatens to use a weapon against you;

10) Forces you to have sex against your will; or
11) Blames you for his or her violent outbursts.

ABORTION LAW

An abortion is one option available to a woman facing an unwanted pregnancy. The Roe vs. Wade decision of the Supreme Court guarantees you this right, with the following limitations. Texas law requires that one parent be informed at least forty-eight hours before a teenager receives an abortion, but the teenager does not need to obtain a parent's permission. There is an alternative by which a teenager can apply to a judge to waive this requirement. This area of law is in a great state of flux. In the spring of 2005, the Supreme Court agreed with the 9th Circuit Court of Appeals in striking down an Idaho law requiring girls under age eighteen to get parental consent for abortions except under the most dire of medical emergencies.

24-HOUR RULE

Texas law presently requires all doctors in the state to warn women seeking an abortion that it may lead to breast cancer. Whether there is a link between abortion and breast cancer is under intense debate in the medical community. The National Cancer Institute, the official government cancer agency, and the American Cancer Society have concluded after consultation with over 100 experts that an abortion "does not increase a woman's subsequent risk of developing breast cancer."

AFTER SIXTEEN WEEKS

In Texas, any abortion after sixteen weeks of pregnancy must be performed in special centers. This requirement is ostensibly for safety reasons, but opponents estimate that it quadruples the cost of such abortions without any significant change in safety.

EMERGENCY CONTRACEPTION

A special dose of commonly prescribed birth control pills, sometimes called the "morning-after pill," can help to prevent pregnancy when taken within three days of a birth-control accident or unprotected sex. It may work by preventing ovulation, fertilization, or implantation, but does not cause an abortion.

> Emergency contraception does not prevent
> HIV or other sexually transmitted diseases.

ALTERNATIVES TO ABORTION

If you become pregnant and are not ready to raise a child, but don't want an abortion either, there are other options. There are nearly 3,000 crisis pregnancy centers throughout the United States that help women find alternatives to abortion. They provide pregnancy tests, counseling, pre- and post-natal medical care, and help women obtain housing, maternity and baby clothes, baby equipment, legal assistance, and financial support.

ADOPTION

Adoption is the primary alternative to either abortion or raising a child. Complex disputes between biological and adoptive parents have garnered a lot of media attention in recent years, but these are the exception. Adoption can be a reassuring alternative to a woman in an unplanned pregnancy.

Adoption is the legal transfer of parental rights from the natural or birth parents to adoptive parents. The adoptive parents become legally responsible for the child and obtain all legal parental rights. A new birth certificate is issued for the child, reflecting the adoptive parents' names. The original is retained, but is sealed and accessible only by court order. Some adoptions take place within a family, known as relative adoptions (for example, by a stepparent, grandparent, aunt or uncle).

Any adult in Texas may file a petition to adopt a child. Most adoptions are to married couples, but in Texas, single, separated, and divorced people have the right to adopt, as well. There are no legal standards for adoption regarding age, housing situation, social background, or income level, and Texas law forbids discrimination in adoption because of race or ethnicity.

The Texas Department of Protective and Regulatory Services is the state adoption agency, but there are many licensed private agencies. Adoption can be as individualized as the birth parents and adoptive parents wish to make it. In all cases, the child's biological parents must sign a document relinquishing all legal rights with regard to the child. There must be an attempt to notify and involve the biological father before the adoption is finalized. The consent of the birth mother may not be obtained until forty-eight hours after the child is born, and it must be witnessed by two people and verified by a notary. Once the birth mother has signed the relinquishment form, it cannot be revoked for sixty days. During this sixty-day period, a judge decides whether to accept the consent form and terminate parental rights. Once the court enters a final adoption order, the new birth certificate is issued and the legal rights and responsibilities of parenting are transferred to the adoptive parents. Then the adoption may not be challenged by the birth parents or any other parties.

It is a third degree felony to offer to buy or sell a baby in Texas, which means that the adoptive parents may not pay a parent or a third person for the right to adopt a child, but are allowed to pay reasonable expenses in connection with the adoption.

ADOPTION RECORDS

Adoptive parents, legal guardians of adopted adults, and adopted adults may obtain non-identifying information about the adoption. Adopted adults, birth parents, and birth siblings age twenty-one or older can obtain information through a registry provided by either the adoption agency or the Texas Department of Health–Bureau of Vital Statistics. An adoptee must petition the court in which the adoption was finalized to obtain the sealed original birth certificate.

WHO'S THE FATHER? ESTABLISHING PATERNITY

When a child is born, the mother's husband is presumed to be the father. This includes common-law marriages and marriages within 300 days before the birth. Why 300 days? This is to take account of situations where the birth mother was married at the time of conception, but the marriage was ended by divorce, annulment, or death during the pregnancy, thus making the ex-husband or deceased husband the presumed father. If someone other than the ex-husband is the biological father, the ex-husband may give up his parental rights by completing the Denial of Paternity section on an Acknowledgment of Paternity (AOP) document. This document asks for the biological father to be established as the legal father and to be listed on the birth certificate; otherwise the husband is the legal father. In order to legally establish paternity in the case of a recently deceased husband who is not the biological father, or where the ex-husband and/or the mother refuses to acknowledge a claim of paternity by another man, the man should contact either an attorney or the office of the Texas attorney general's Child Support Program to obtain a court order naming the biological father as the legal father of the baby.

If the mother was not married at the time of the birth, or within 300 days before the birth, by law there is no presumed father and any man claiming to be the father, with the mother's consent, may establish paternity by executing an AOP form either at birth or anytime thereafter. This can also be done if the father is in a foreign country, in the military, or otherwise indisposed, by sending an AOP form to him for his signature and completion.

If a man believes he is the father of the child, but the mother disagrees or her husband refuses to release his paternity rights, a Notice of Intent to Claim Paternity may be filed by the man claiming to be the father. This asserts that he believes he is the father and wishes to preserve his rights as a parent. He should then contact either an attorney or the office of the Texas attorney general's Child Support Program to obtain a court order naming him the legal father of the baby.

WHY SHOULD I ESTABLISH PATERNITY FOR MY CHILD?

Most people are of the opinion that all children should at least know who their biological father is, no matter who raises them. Also, the establishment of paternity is an essential step in getting court-ordered child support payments. Further, the child may be entitled to government benefits through the father, such as Social Security, veteran's benefits and health care insurance. Finally, knowing the biological father and his family medical history may provide helpful and sometimes vital information for future medical treatment.

FATHERS' RIGHTS

Once the legal father is either established by circumstance or determined by a court of law, he becomes a natural guardian of the minor child and has the right to take legal action on behalf of the child in certain circumstances. A paternity case is a lawsuit to determine the natural and legal father of a minor child and to confer on him the rights and duties of a parent. Once an individual has been determined to be the biological father, he obtains rights such as visitation, and also the obligations for financial support. The mother of the child must consult with the father about such subjects as the child's religious upbringing, education, medical care, and vacations. An unmarried biological father has the same rights as a married father, including the right to obtain custody of the minor child if appropriate, and to have a say in how the child is raised and cared for.

CHILD SUPPORT

Any parent not having custody of a child is at least responsible to financially assist in supporting that child. The Texas Family Code contains guidelines for the computation of child support, which are designed for situations in which the obligor's monthly net resources are $6,000 or less. Generally speaking, the amount of child support owed is according to the following formula:

1 child	20% of payor's net resources
2 children	25% of payor's net resources
3 children	30% of payor's net resources
4 children	35% of payor's net resources
5 children	40% of payor's net resources
6+ children	not less than 40% of payor's net resources

If there are children from other relationships, the percentages listed above may be reduced by the court, and if the noncustodial parent's net resources exceed $6,000 per month, the court may order additional amounts of child support, depending on the situation. The noncustodial parent is also required to maintain the children on his or her employment-sponsored health insurance policy, or to pay the amount necessary to maintain insurance coverage if it is available and affordable.

Child support orders and obligations generally continue until the child reaches age eighteen or graduates from high school. In the event a child is disabled, child support may continue indefinitely. All orders relating to the child support and custody may be modified by the court or by agreement between the parties, but remember that informal agreements are not legally binding. If such an agreement is reached, contact an attorney to have the court enter an order pursuant to the agreement; otherwise someone may be in violation of the court's orders.

An unmarried biological father has the same rights as a married father, including the right to obtain custody of the minor child if appropriate, and to have a say in how the child is raised and cared for.

Orders for child support payments are enforceable, and failure to pay can result in garnishment of wages and tax refunds, and even imprisonment. Even if visitation is being denied by the custodial parent, child support payments

The Student Body of Law

must continue. Visitation and child support payments are separate issues; if a court order on either is violated, contact an attorney to seek sanctions from the court.

The Texas Attorney General's office is the official child support enforcement agency for the state of Texas, and provides services for parents seeking support for their children. The Child Support Division determines, on a case-by-case basis, which of the following child support services are appropriate: locating a noncustodial parent; establishing paternity; establishing and enforcing child or medical support orders; and reviewing, adjusting, collecting and distributing child support payments. Contact the Texas attorney general's office for more information at (800) 252-8014 or www.oag.state.tx.us.

CONCLUSION

As I said at the beginning of this book, knowledge is power. The more you know, the better prepared you are to deal with whatever situation you find yourself in. I hope that this book has answered some of your questions. Although it is not intended as legal advice, it should give you some insight into the law in various situations and help you conduct yourself lawfully. But please do not use your knowledge of the law as a tool to take advantage of anyone. The laws of our state are intended to promote fairness for everyone, and to make sure that people know what they should do in ambiguous situations.

If you are unsure about your rights, the law, or how to get something done, contact an attorney for help. Most reputable lawyers will sit down and talk with you at no charge to at least determine what help you need. Your school may have an attorney on staff for that purpose.

With the knowledge gained from reading this book, I hope you will avoid some of the pitfalls that many college students and young adults fall into. So work, study, and play hard; enjoy your time in college, and if you take advantage of this great time in your life, you should enjoy a successful future, whatever you choose to do with it.

INDEX

A

Abortion	187,188
Accident	74,78,79,132,133,139,141,142,145-148,150,176,187
Adoption	188,189
Alcohol	21,27,36,45,59,61-69,74-81,104,115-116,140,174,179 184,186
Arrest & Bail	39
Assault	5,6,15,27,28,29,30,31,37,37,44,45,59,78,88,88-89,109 113,141,173,175,181-182,184

B

Bicycle	151-153
Birth Control	181,187
Boats	74,104-107

C

Camping	103
Checks	19,27,116,122,154,156,159,160,167-168
Child Support	115,142,190-192
Cigarettes	38,58
Civil Liability	61
Computer Crimes	92-93
Concealed Handgun License	115
Consent	20,22-23,79,89-90,92,101,126,150,175,177181-182,184 186-190
Consent to Search	20,22-23
Conspiracy	28,38-39
Controlled Substances	83-84,86
Credit Cards	154,156-158,162
Crimes of Moral Turpitude	27
Crimina Record	32-35,40,47

D

Deadly Force	6,108-113
Deferred Adjudication	25-26,29,35,36,77,145
Drinking Age	69
Driver Points	145

Driver's License   11,30,32,51,58-59,71-72,74,78-80,100,105,124 140-150,165,17
Drug-Free Zone   85-86
Drugs   20,26,36,67,69,82,84-85,87,89,98,162,181,185,186
DWI   12,59,69,73-80,104,140-141,143,145,174

E

Eviction   122-123
Expunction   34-36

F

Facilitating Escape   6
Failure to Identify   71-72
Fake ID   72,174-175
Felony   5,6,15-26,34,37,38,41,50,73,77-78,83-88,93-94,96,109 115,141,159,168,172-178,189
Filing Charges   44
First Amendment   15-18,94
Fishing   100-101
Free Speech   15-17

G

Gambling   28,99-100
Guilt by Association   168
Guns   20,97,108,113-114,144

H

Hazing   95-96
Helmet Law   149
Hunting   74,100,101-102,114

I

Identification   10-11,51,58,71,77,100,105,132,165
Indecent Exposure   29,30,88,91,98,99
Insurance   54,58,74,77-78,132-134,138,139,141,142,144,146-150 162,175,190-191

J

Jury Duty   49,51-53
Juvenile Record   36-37,47

L

Lawyers   2,8-9,43-44,51,144-145,193

The Student Body of Law

Lease	114,118-125,128-129
Legally Intoxicated	74
Liens	130-131

M

Miranda Warning	10
Misdemeanor	5-6,20,25-27,34,36-37,39,63,71-73,77,80,82-86 91,93-99,109,115,127,161,169,170-174,176-178
Motorcycle	58,130,149-151
Moving	27,58,119,121,123-124,141,143,145,152
Moving Violations	27,141,143

N

Noise	27,60,61,103-104,169

O

Organ Donor	150
Organized Criminal Activity	39

P

Parking	62,71,74,97,110,112,128,129,134-139,153
Passport	162,164-167
Police	4-7,10-12,14-15,19,21-22,26-27,32,33,38,40,61,63,70,72 74,78,81,82,85,91,95,98,117,127,135,139,144,147,148,171,173 183,186
Porn	94
Probably Cause	20
Probation	25-26,29-31,35,41,45,73,80,160
Protective Order	36,45,115
Public Intoxication	31,63,81,82
Public Lewdness	91
Public Nudity	92,98

R

Rape	77,110,181,183-186
Reasonable Suspicion	19-20
Resisting Arrest	5,109
Right to Remain Silent (Fifth Amendment)	10-11,14,40,77
Roadside Tests	75
Roommates	124-125,160,173

S

Sales Agreement	131

Search and Seizure   19,22
Security Deposit   123-124,142
Selective Service   54-57
Self-Defense   108,116
Sex   15,26,28-31,33,36,48-49,52,68,87,91,98-99,180,182-184,187
Sex Crimes   28-29,98-99
Solicitation of a Minor   90
Speeding   27,42,68,72,85,141,143-145
SR-22   134,141-143
Subpoena   13,43

T

Titles   102,131
Tow   128,134-139
Travel   53,130,144-145,162-166
Trespassing   27,100,103,126-128
Trial   10,12-13,15,32,43-44,49-50,53,76,78-79,109,144-145,174

V

Victim's Rights   44
Voting   47-49,116

W

Warrant   13,20-23,27,42,70,72,104,124,159-160
Weapons   36,97,108,111,113,117

Y

Your Home   21,23,48,60,70,110
Your Vehicle   5,23,76,146-147

About the Author

Scot Courtney received a Bachelor of Arts Degree with a double major from Southwest Texas State University in 1990 and his law degree from Thurgood Marshall School of Law, where he was a distinguished senior staff member of Law Review and graduated with honors.

Scot is also a member of the Association of Trial Lawyers of America, Harris County Criminal Defense Lawyer's Association, Travis County Criminal Defense Lawyer's Association, Texas Criminal Defense Lawyer's Association, as well as MENSA and has been recognized as one of the Top Lawyers of Houston by the readers, editors and staff of H Texas magazine.

The Student Body of Law is his first book.

We're Still Here: Contemporary Virginia Indians Tell Their Stories
Sandra Wauagaman & Danielle Moretti-Langholtz, Ph.D.
ISBN 1928662013, $14.95, paperback

Just updated for 2006 to include:
-Jamestown 2007
-Werowocomoco
-National Museum of the American Indian
-Teacher's resource guide

"This book fills a void...It covers all of the tribes, and is informative, but easy to read."
—Joyce Krigsvold, Paumunkey Indian Museum

The 7 Most Powerful Selling Secrets
John Livesay
ISBN 1928662048, $19.95, hardcover

""John Livesay's book identifies three critical ingredients to mastering the 'art of salesmanship' for today's business world - your voice, your energy, and your soul. John's unique insights into humanizing the sales experience makes this book a "must-read" for newcomers, as well as seasoned vets. If you are looking for opportunities to update your tools of the trade and gain a competitive advantage in the sales arena, then look no further than this book!"
—Kevin Carroll, Creative Motivator to Nike designers (aka The Katalyst), Nike

Poor Man's Philanthropist: The Thomas Cannon Story
Sandra Waugaman with Thomas *Cannon*
ISBN 1928662056, $23.95, hardcover

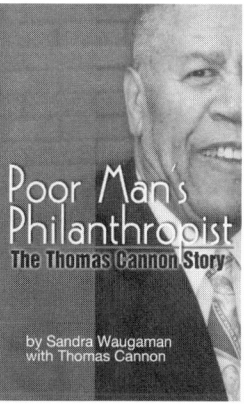

Thomas Cannon (referred to as "The Poor Man's Philanthropist) was a retired postal worker of modest means who awarded gifts of $1,000 to deserving individuals. Over the past three decades, Cannon, a retired postal worker, had given $146,000, usually in $1,000 checks, to individuals he felt were setting an example for others. Read about his inspiring life story.

"Cannon is now a legend in Richmond."
—Parade Magazine

BUY DIRECT FROM PALARI

Save with free shipping on these titles.

The Student Body of Law for Texas

Scot Courtney

(ISBN-10: 1-928662-09-9)

$14.95, trade paperback

Remember FREE SHIPPING when ordered with this form!

Deliver books to:

Name_____

Phone_____-_____ Email_____

Address_____

City_____ State_____ Zip_____

                                                                          Number of Books   Total

We're Still Here $14.95 @ _____ = _____

The 7 Selling Secrets $19.95 @ _____ = _____

Poor Man's Philanthropist $23.95 @ _____ = _____

The Student Body of Law $14.95 @ _____ = _____

VA residents add 5.0% sales tax = _____

TOTAL ENCLOSED = _____

Order online at WWW.PALARIBOOKS.com
or send check or money order to
Palari Publishing
P. O. Box 9288
Richmond, Virginia 23227-0288